MARY SLESSOR THE WHITE QUEEN

MARY SLESSOR

"One of the best books I ever read. . . Mary is worthy to stand beside and before Santa Teresa herself for distinction and originality and devotion and prayer and work."—DR. ALEXANDER WHYTE.

"I have been thrilled by a book called *Mary Slessor*. I think the plain prosaic story told by Mr. Livingstone is more enthralling than any æsthetic impression of tropical evil."—JAMES DOUGLAS.

"*Mary Slessor* is a book to buy, to read, and to lend—but also to recover, for it is a book one will want to turn to again and again."—*Challenge*.

"One of the most remarkable narratives of missionary life that has been published for some time. The story of missions does not lack heroines, but the record has no one quite like Mary Slessor. Her courage was marvellous."—*Westminster Gazette*.

MARY SLESSOR
THE WHITE QUEEN

A TRUE STORY OF ADVENTURE,
HEROISM AND FAITH

BY
W. P. LIVINGSTONE

HODDER AND STOUGHTON
LIMITED LONDON

First Published in this Form *April 1931*
Nineteenth impression *1960*

Originally Published as
"The White Queen of Okoyong."

CONTENTS

CHAPTER V

CHAPTER VI

CHAPTER VII

CHAPTER VIII

CHAPTER IX

My life, my all, Lord, I entreat,
  Take, and use, and make replete
With the love and patience sweet
  That made *Thy* life so complete.

MARY SLESSOR.

CHIEF DATES IN MISS SLESSOR'S LIFE

YEAR		PAGE
1848.	Born at Gilcomston, Aberdeen, December 2.	
1856.	Family went to Dundee.	13
1859.	Began work in a factory.	14
1876.	Appointed by United Presbyterian Church to Calabar as missionary teacher, and sailed.	22 and 23
1879.	Paid her first visit home.	27
1880.	In charge at Old Town.	27
1883.	Second visit home with Janie.	33
1885.	In Creek Town.	34
1886.	Death of her mother and sister (Janie).	34
1888.	Entered Okoyong alone.	38
1891.	Third visit home with Janie.	58
1892.	Made Government Agent in Okoyong.	61
1898.	Fourth visit home, with Janie, Alice, Maggie, and Mary.	73
1900.	Union of United Presbyterian and Free Churches as United Free Church.	92
1902.	Pioneering in Enyong Creek.	90
1903.	Started a Mission at Itu. Reached Arochuku.	89
1904.	Settled at Itu.	90
1905.	Settled at Ikotobong.	91
	Appointed Vice-President of Native Court.	93
1907.	Fifth visit home with Dan.	96
	Settled at Use.	98
1908.	Began a home for women and girls.	101
1909.	Gave up Court work.	88
1910.	Began work at Ikpe.	104
1912.	Holiday at Grand Canary.	107
1913.	Visit to Okoyong.	110
	Received Royal Medal.	112
	Began work at Odoro Ikpe.	114
1914.	Last illness, August.	122
1915.	Died at Use, January 13.	123

CHAPTER I

Tells how a little girl lived in a lowly home, and played, and dreamed dreams, and how a dark shadow came into her life and made her unhappy; how when she grew older she went into a factory and learned to weave, and how in her spare minutes she taught herself many things, and worked amongst wild boys; and how she was sent to Africa.

ONE cold day in December, in the city of Aberdeen, a baby girl was carried by her mother into a church to be enrolled in the Kingdom of Jesus and given a name. As the minister went through the tender and beautiful ceremony the people in the pews looked at the tiny form in her robes of white, and thought of the long years that lay before her and wondered what she would become, because every girl and boy is like a shut casket full of mystery and promise and hope. No one knows what gifts may lie hidden within them, and what great and surprising things they may do when they grow up and go out into the world.

Then the minister sprinkled a little water on the face of the child and called her "Mary Slessor," and she was carried out and wrapped up carefully again and taken home.

It was not a very fine house into which Mary had been born, for her father, who was a shoemaker, did not earn much money; but her mother, a sweet and gentle woman, worked hard to keep it clean and tidy, and love makes even the poorest place sunshiny and warm. When Mary was able to run about she played a great deal with her brother Robert, who was older than she, but she liked to help her mother too: indeed she seemed to be fonder of doing things for others than for herself. She did not need dolls, for more babies came into the home, and she used to nurse them and dress them and hush them to sleep.

She was very good at make-believe, and one of her games was to sit in a corner and pretend that she was keeping school. If you had listened to her you would have found that the pupils she was busy teaching and keeping in order were children with skins as black as coal. The reason was this. Her mother took a great interest in all she heard on Sundays about the dark lands beyond the seas where millions of people had never heard of Jesus. The church to which she belonged, the United Presbyterian Church, had sent out many brave men and women to various parts of the world to fight the evils of heathenism, and a new Mission had just begun amongst a savage race in a wild country called Calabar in West Africa, and every one in Scotland was talking about it and the perils and hardships of the missionaries. Mrs. Slessor used to come home with all the news about the work, and the children would gather about her knees and listen to stories of the strange cruel customs of the natives, and how they killed the twin-babies, until their eyes grew big and round, and their hearts raced with fear, and they snuggled close to her side.

Mary was very sorry for these helpless bush-children, and often thought about them, and that was why she made them her play-scholars. She dreamed, too, of going out some day to that terrible land and saving the lives of the twinnies, and sometimes she would look up and say :

" Mother, I want to be a missionary and go out and teach the black boys and girls—real ways."

Then Robert would retort in the tone that boys often use to their sisters :

" But you're only a girl, and girls can't be missionaries. *I'm* going to be one and you can come out with me, and if you're good I may let you up into my pulpit beside me."

Mrs. Slessor was amused at their talk, and well pleased too, for she had a longing that her boy should work abroad in the service of Jesus when he became a man. But that was not to be, for soon afterwards Robert fell ill and died, so Mary became the eldest.

A dark shadow, darker than death, gathered over the home. Mr. Slessor learned the habit of taking strong drink and became a slave to it, and he began to spend a large part of his money in the public-house, and his wife and children had not the comfort they ought to have had. Matters became so bad that something had to be done. It was thought that if Mr. Slessor could be got away from the bad companions who led him astray, he might do better.

So the home was broken up, and the family journeyed to Dundee, the busy, smoky town on the River Tay, where there were many large mills and factories, and here, for a time, they lived in a little house with a bit of garden in front. That garden was at first a delight to Mary, but afterwards she lost her pleasure in it, for her father used to dig in it on Sunday, and make people think he did not love God's Day.

She was now old enough to look after the younger children, and very well she did it. Often she took them long walks, climbing the steep streets to see the green fields, or going down to feel the fresh smell of the sea. Sometimes her mother gave her a sixpence, and they went and had a ride on the merry-go-round. It was the custom then for girls and boys to go bare-footed in the summer, and Mary liked it so much that she never afterwards cared to wear shoes and stockings.

On Sundays they all trotted away to church, clean and sweet, each with a peppermint to suck during the sermon, and afterwards they went to Sunday School. As a rule Mary was good and obedient, though, like most girls, she sometimes got into trouble. Her hair was reddish then, and her brothers would tease her and call her "Carrots," and she did not like that. She loved a prank too, and was sometimes naughty. Once or twice she played truant from the Sunday School. She was always very vexed afterwards, for she could not bear to see her mother's face when she heard of her wrong-doing—it was so white and sad. The quiet little mother did not punish her: she would draw her instead into a room and kneel down and pray for her. "Oh, mother!" Mary would say, "I would rather you whip me!"

But all that soon passed away, for she had been dreaming another dream, a very sweet one, which always set her heart a-longing and a-thrilling, and it now came true and changed her life. It was the biggest thing and the happiest that ever happened to her. She gave her heart to Jesus. Very shyly one night she crept up to her mother, nestled close to her, and laid her head on her knee, and then whispered the wonderful news. "I'll try, mother," she said, "to be a good girl and a comfort to you." Her mother was filled with joy, and both went about for long afterwards singing in their hearts. If only the shadow would lift!

But it settled down more darkly than ever. We can change the place where we stay and wander far, but it is not so easy to change our habits. Mr. Slessor was now bringing in so little money that his wife was forced to go and work in one of the mills in order to buy food and clothes for the children. Mary became the little house-mother, and how busy her hands and feet were, how early she was up, and how late she tumbled into bed, and how bravely she met all her troubles! Tears might steal into her eyes when she felt faint and hungry, but it was always a bright and smiling face that welcomed the tired mother home at night.

Gloomier grew the shadow. More money was needed to keep the home, and Mary, a slim girl of eleven, was the next to go out and become a bread-winner. One morning she went into a big factory and stood in the midst of machines and wheels and whirling belts, and at first was bewildered and a little afraid. But she was only allowed to stay for half a day: the other half she had to go to a school in the works where the girls were taught to read and write and count. She was fond of the reading, but did not like doing the sums: the figures on the board danced before her eyes, and she could not follow the working out of the problems, and sometimes the teacher punished her by making her stand until the lesson was finished.

But she was clever with her fingers, and soon knew all about weaving. How proud she was when she ran home with her first week's earnings! She laid them in the lap of her mother, who cried over them and wrapped them up and put them away: she could not, just then, find it in her heart to spend such precious money.

By the time she was fourteen Mary was working a large machine and being paid a good wage. But she had to toil very hard for it. She rose at five o'clock in the morning, when the factory whistle blew, and was in the works by six, and, except for two hours off for meals, she was busy at her task until six in the evening. In the warm summer days she did not go home, but carried her dinner with her and ate it sitting beside the loom; and sometimes she went away by herself and walked in the park. Saturday afternoons and Sundays were her own, but they were usually spent in helping her mother. Her dress was coarse and plain, and she wore no pretty ornaments, though she liked them as much as her companions did, for she was learning to put aside all the things she did not really need, and by and by she came not to miss them, and found pleasure instead in making others happy. She would have been quite content if only her father had been different.

But there was no hope now of a better time. The shadow became so black that it was like night when there are no stars in the sky. Mrs. Slessor and Mary had a big burden to bear and a grim battle to fight. In their distress they clung to one another, and prayed to Jesus for help and strength, for they, of themselves, could do little. On Saturday nights Mr. Slessor came home late, and treated them unkindly, so that Mary was often forced to go out into the cold streets and wait until he had gone to sleep. As she wandered about she felt very lonely and very miserable, and sometimes sobbed as if her heart would break. When she passed the bright windows of the places where drink was sold, she wondered why people were allowed to ruin men and women in such a way, and she clenched her hands and resolved that when she grew up she would war against this terrible thing which destroyed the peace and happiness of homes.

But at last the trouble came to an end. One tragic day Mary stood and looked down with a great awe upon the face of her father lying white and still in death.

What she went through in these days made her often sad and downcast, for she had a loving heart, and suffered sorely when any one was rough to her or ill-treated her. But good came out of it too. She was like a white starry flower which grows on the walls and verandahs of houses in the tropics. The hot sunshine is not able to draw perfume from it, but as soon as darkness falls its fragrance scents the air and comes stealing through the open windows and doors. So it was with Mary. She grew sweeter in the darkness of trouble ; it was in the shadows of life that she learned to be patient and brave and unselfish.

We must not think less, but more, of her for coming out of such a home. It is not always the girls and boys who are highly favoured that grow up to do the best and biggest things in life. Some of the men and women to whom the world owes most had a hard time when they were young. The home life of President Lincoln, who freed millions of slaves in America, was like Mary's, yet his name has become one of the most famous in history. No girl or boy should despair because they are poor or lonely or crushed down in any way ; let them fight on, quietly and patiently, and in the end better things and happier times will come.

Mrs. Slessor now left the factory, and for a time kept a little shop, in which Mary used to help, especially on Saturday afternoons and nights, when trade was busiest. The girl was still dreaming dreams about the wonderful days that lay before her, but, unlike many others who do the same she did her best to make hers come true. She wanted to learn things, and she found that books would tell her, and so she was led into the great world of knowledge. The more she read the more she wanted to know. So eager was she that when she left home for her work, she slipped a book into her pocket and glanced at it in the streets. She did not know then about Dr. Livingstone, the African missionary and traveller, but she did exactly what he had done when he was a boy : she propped a book on a corner of the loom in the factory, and read whenever she had a moment to spare. Her companions tell how they used to see her take out a little note-book, put it on the weaver's beam, and jot down her thoughts—she was always writing, they say ; sometimes it was poetry, sometimes an essay, sometimes a letter to a friend. But she never neglected her work.

How different her lot was from that of most girls of to-day ! They have leisure for their lessons, and they learn music and do fancy work and keep house and bake—and how many hate it all ! Mary had only a few precious minutes, but she made the most of them. The books she read were not stories, but ones like Milton's *Paradise Lost* and Carlyle's *Sartor Resartus*, and so deep did she become in them at night that sometimes she forgot everything, and read on and on through the quiet hours, and only came to herself with a start when she heard the warning whistle of the factory in the early morning.

She was fond of all good books, but the one she liked most and knew better than any was the Bible. She pored over it so often that she remembered much of it by heart. In the Bible Class she was so quick and so ready to answer questions that Mr. Baxter, her minister, used to say, "Now, Mary Slessor, don't answer any more questions till I bid you." When every one else failed he would turn to her with "Now, Mary," and she always had her reply ready. She was never tired of the story of Jesus, especially as it is told in the Gospel of St. John, for there He appeared to her so kind and winsome and lovable. When she thought of all He did, how He came from His own beautiful heaven to save the world from what is sinful and sad, and how He was made to suffer and at last was put to death, and how His teaching has brought peace and safety and sunshine into the lives of millions of women and girls, she felt she must do something for Him to show her love and thankfulness and devotion.

"He says we must do as He did and try to make people better and happier, and so I, too, must do my best and join in the war against all that is evil and unlovely and unrestful in the world." So she thought to herself.

She did not say, "I am only a girl, what can I do?" She knew that when a General wanted an army to fight a strong enemy he did not call for officers only, but for soldiers—hosts of them, and especially for those who were young. "I can be a soldier," Mary said humbly. "Dear Lord, I will do what I can—here are my heart and head and hands and feet—use me for anything that I can do."

The first thing that she did was to take a class of little girls in the Sunday School, and thus she began to teach others before she was educated herself, but it is not always those who are best trained who can teach best. The heart of Mary was so full of deep true love for Jesus that it caused her face to shine and her eyes to smile and her lips to speak kind words, and that is the sort of learning that wins others to Him.

Wishart Church, to which she went, was built over shops, and looked down upon the old Port Gate and upon streets and lanes which were filled at night with big boys and girls who seemed to have no other place to go to, and nothing to do but lounge and swear and fight. Mary felt she would like to do something for them. By and by when a Mission was begun in a little house in Queen Street—there is a brass inscription upon the wall, now, telling about Mary—she went to the superintendent and said: "Will you take me as a teacher?" "Gladly," he said, but she looked so small and frail that he was afraid the work would be too rough for her.

What a time she had at first! The boys and girls did not want anybody to bother about them: those who came to the meeting were wild and noisy; those who remained outside threw stones and mud and tried to stop the work. Mary faced them, smiling and unafraid, and dared them to touch her. Some grew ashamed of worrying the brave little teacher, and these she won over to her side. But there were others with sullen eyes and clenched fists who would not give in, and they did their best to make her life a misery.

One night a band of the most violent lay in wait for her, and she found herself suddenly in their midst. They hustled and threatened her.

"We'll do for you if you don't leave us alone," they cried.

She was quaking with fear, but she did not show it. She just breathed a prayer for help, and looked at them with her quiet eyes.

"I will not give up," she replied. "You can do what you like."

"All right," shouted the leader, a big hulking lad. "Here goes."

Out of his pocket he took a lump of lead to which was tied a bit of cord, and began to swing it round her head. The rest of the gang looked on breathless, wondering at the courage of the girl. The lead came nearer and swished past her brow. Pale, calm, unflinching, she stood waiting for the blow that would fell her to the ground. Suddenly the lad jerked away the weapon and let it fall with a crash.

"We can't force her, boys," he cried, "she's game."

And, like beaten foes, they followed her, and went to the meeting and into her class, and after that there was no more trouble. The boys fell under her spell, grew fond of her, and in their shy way did all they could to help her. On Saturday afternoons she would take them into the country away from the temptations of the streets, and sought to make them gentle and kind and generous. Some of the most wayward amongst them gave their hearts to Jesus, and afterwards grew to be good and useful men.

What was it that gave her such an influence over these rude and unruly boys? They did not know. She was not what is called a pretty girl. She was plain and quiet and simple, and she was poorly clad. But she was somehow different from most teachers. Perhaps it was because she loved them so much, for the love that is real and pure and unselfish is the greatest power in the world.

Through the hearts of the boys Mary found her way to their homes in the slums, and paid visits to their mothers and sisters, and saw that life to them was often very hard and wretched. The other Mission workers used to go two and two, but she often went alone. Once she was a long time away, and when she came back she said laughingly:

"I've been dining with the Macdonalds in Quarry Pend."

"Indeed," said some one, "and did you get a clean plate and spoon?"

"Oh, never mind that," replied Mary. "I've got into their house and been asked to come back, and that's all I care about."

She always went in the same spirit in which Jesus would have gone. Sometimes she would sit by the fire with the baby on her knees; sometimes she would take tea with the family, drinking out of a broken cup; sometimes she would help the mother to finish a bit of work. And always she cheered up tired and anxious hearts, and left sunshine and peace where there had been only the blackness of despair.

No one could be long in her company without feeling better, and not a few of her friends came, through her, to know and love and work for Jesus.

"Three weeks after I knew her," says one of her old factory mates, "I became a different girl." How eager and earnest she was! "Oh!" she said to a companion, "I wonder what we would do or dare for Jesus? Would we be burned at the stake? Would we give our lives for His sake?" "She *did* work hard," says another, "and whatever she did, she did with heart and soul."

When the Mission was removed to the rooms under the church, the superintendent said: "We shall need a charwoman to give the place a thorough cleaning."

"Nonsense," said Mary; "we will clean it ourselves."

"You ladies clean such a dirty hall!"

"Ladies!" cried Mary; "we are no ladies, we are just ordinary working folk."

Next night Mary and another teacher were found with sleeves turned up and aprons on, busy with pails of water and brushes scrubbing out the rooms.

Like other young people, she had her troubles, big and little, and these she met bravely. Evil-minded persons, jealous of her goodness, sometimes said unkind things about her, but she never paid any heed to them. She always did what she thought was right, and went her own way. On Saturdays she used to put her hair in curlpapers, and her companions teased her a lot about it, and tried to laugh her out of the habit, but she just laughed back. When she and two or three friends met during the meal hour and held a little prayer-meeting opposite the factory the other girls would come and peep in, and one of her companions would be vexed and scold them. "Dinna bother, Janet," she would say quietly, "we needna mind what they do."

She was not always serious, but could enjoy fun and frolic with the wildest. Once while walking in the country with a girl she knocked playfully at some cottage doors and ran away. "Oh, Mary," said her friend, "I'm shocked at you!"

Mary only laughed and said: "A little nonsense now and then is relished by the wisest men."

From one old friend we get a picture of her at this time. "Her face was always shining and happy. With her fresh skin, her short ringlets, and her firm mouth she somehow always made me think of a farmer's daughter coming to market with butter and eggs!"

Her life during these years was a training for what she had to do in the future. She must have had an inkling of it, for her dreams now were all of service in the far lands beyond the seas. Through the gloom of the smoky streets she was always seeing visions of tropical rivers and tangled jungle and heathen huts amongst palm trees, and above the noise of the factory she was hearing the cries of the little bush-children; and she longed to leave busy Dundee with its churches and Sunday Schools and go out and help where help was most needed. She did not say anything, for she knew it was her brother John that her mother was anxious to make a missionary. He was a big lad, but very delicate, and there came a time when the doctor said he must leave the cold climate of Scotland or die. He sailed to New Zealand, but it was too late, and he passed away there. His mother grieved again over her lost hopes, and Mary, who was very fond of him, wept bitterly. As she went about her work she repeated the hymn, "Lead, kindly Light," to herself, finding comfort in the last two lines:

> And with the morn those angel faces smile
> Which I have loved long since, and lost awhile.

And then she came back to her dazzling day-dream. Could she not, after all, be the missionary? But she was not educated, and she was the chief breadwinner of the family, and her mother leant upon her so much. How could she manage it? She thought it all out, and at last said, "I *can* do it. I *will* do it." She was one of the cleverest weavers in the factory, and she began to do extra work, thus earning a bigger wage and saving more money. She studied very hard. She practised speaking at meetings until she learned how to put her thoughts into clear and simple words.

But it was a weary, weary time, for she spent fourteen years within the walls of the factory. Thousands of other girls, of course, were doing the same, and sometimes they got very tired, but had just to go bravely on. In one of her poems Mrs. Browning tells us what it was like: how the revolving wheels seemed to make everything turn too—the heads and hearts of the girls, the walls, the sky seen out of the high windows, even the black flies on the ceiling—

> All day, the iron wheels are droning,
> And sometimes we could pray,
> "O ye wheels" (breaking out in a mad moaning),
> "Stop! be silent for to-day!"

But they never did stop, and the girls had only their hopes and dreams to make them patient and brave.

One day there flashed through the land a telegram which caused much excitement and sorrow. Africa was then an unknown country, vast and mysterious, and haunted by all the horrors of slavery and heathenism. For a long time there had been tramping through it a white man, a Scotsman, David Livingstone, hero of heroes, who had been gradually finding out the secrets of its lakes and rivers and peoples. Sometimes he was lost for years. The telegram which came told of his lonely death in a hut in the heart of the continent Every one asked: What is to be done now? who is to take up the work of the great pioneer and help to save the natives from misery and death? Amongst those whose hearts leapt at the call was Mary Slessor. She went to her mother.

"Mother," she said, "I am going to offer myself as a missionary. But do not fret. I will be able to give you part of my salary, and that, with the earnings of Susan and Janie, will keep the home in comfort."

"My lassie," was the reply, "I'll willingly let you go. You'll make a fine missionary, and I'm sure God will be with you."

Some of her friends wondered at her. They knew she was not specially brave; indeed, was not her timidity a joke amongst them? "Why," they said, "she is even afraid of dogs. When she sees one coming down the street she goes into a passage until it is past!" This was true, but they forgot that love can cast out all fear.

Tremblingly she waited for the answer to her letter to the Mission Board of the United Presbyterian Church in Edinburgh. When it arrived she rushed to her mother.

"I'm accepted! I'm going to Calabar as a teacher." And then, strange to say, she burst into tears.

So she who had waited so long and so patiently, working within the walls of a factory, weaving the warp and woof in the loom, was now going to one of the wildest parts of Africa to weave there the lives of the people into new and beautiful patterns.

CHAPTER II

How our heroine sailed away to a golden land of sunshine across the sea; how she found that under all the beauty there were terrible things which made life a misery to the dark-skinned natives; how she began to fight their evil ideas and ways and to rescue little children from death; how, after losing all her loved ones, she took a little twin-girl to her heart, and how she grew strong and calm and brave.

On an autumn morning in 1876 Miss Slessor stood on the deck of the steamer *Ethiopia* in Liverpool docks and waved good-bye to two companions from Dundee who had gone to see her off. As the vessel cleared the land and moved out into the wide spaces of the waters she, who had always lived in narrow streets, felt as if she were on holiday, and was in as high spirits as any schoolgirl. She could not help being kind and helpful to others, and soon made friends with many of the passengers and crew.

One man drew her like a magnet, for he also was a dreamer of dreams. This was Mr. Thomson, an architect from Glasgow, who was filled with the idea that the missionaries in West Africa would do better work and remain out longer if there were some cool place near at hand to which they could go for a rest and change. He had been all over the Coast, and explored the rivers and hills, and had at last found a healthy spot five thousand feet up on the Cameroon Mountains, where he decided to build a home. He had given up his business, and was now on his way out, with his wife and two workmen, to put his dream into shape. Mary's eyes shone as she listened to his tale of love and sacrifice; but, alas! the plan, so beautiful, so full of hope for the missionaries, came to nothing, for he died not long after landing.

It was from Mr. Thomson that she learned most about the strange country to which she was going. He told her how it was covered with thick bush and forest; how swift, mud-coloured rivers came out of mysterious lands which had never been seen by white men; how the sun shone like a furnace-fire, and how sudden hurricanes of rain and wind came and swept away huts and uprooted trees. He described the wild animals he had seen—huge hippopotami and crocodiles in the creeks; elephants, leopards, and snakes in the forest; and lovely hued birds that flashed in the sunlight—until her eyes sparkled and her cheeks flushed as they had done in the old days when she listened to the stories told by her mother.

Within a week the steamer had passed out of the grey north, and was gliding through a calm sea beneath a blue and sunny sky. By and by Mary was seeking cool corners under the awning, and listening lazily to the swish of the waves from the bows and watching golden sunsets and big bright stars. Sometimes she saw scores of flying-fish hurry-scurrying over the shining surface, and at night the prow of the vessel went flashing through water that sparkled like diamonds.

By and by came the hot smell of Africa, long lines of surf rolling on lonely shores, white fortresses that spoke of the old slave days, and little port towns, half-hidden amongst trees, where she got her first glimpses of the natives, and was amused at the din they made as they came off to the steamer, fearless of the sharks that swarmed in the water. It was all strange and unreal to the Scottish weaver-girl.

And when, after a month, the vessel came to the Calabar River and steamed through waters crowded with white cranes and pelicans, and past dark mangrove swamps and sandbanks where the crocodiles lay sunning themselves, and islands gay with parrots and monkeys, up to Duke Town, the queer huddle of mud huts amongst the palm trees that was to be her home, she was excited beyond telling. For at last that wonderful dream of hers, which she had cherished through so many long years, had come true, and so wonderful was it that it seemed to be still only a dream and nothing more.

Clear above the river and the town, like a lighthouse on a cliff, stood the Mission where "Daddy" and "Mammy" Anderson, two of its famous pioneers, lived, and with them Mary stayed until she knew something about the natives and her work. She felt very happy; she loved the glowing sunshine, the gorgeous sunsets, the white moonlight, the shining river, the flaming blossoms amongst which the humming-birds and butterflies flitted, and all the sights and sounds that were so different from those in Scotland. She was so glad that she used to write poems, and in one of these she sings of the beauty of the land :

> . . . the shimmering, dancing wavelets
> And the stately, solemn palms,
> The wild, weird chant of the boatmen
> And the natives' evening psalms,
> The noise of myriad insects
> And the firefly's soft bright sheen,
> The bush with its thousand terrors
> And its never-fading green.

Her spirits, so long bottled up in Dundee, overflowed, and she did things which amused and sometimes vexed the older and more serious missionaries. She climbed trees and ran races with the black girls and boys, and was so often late at meals that Mrs. Anderson, by way of punishment, left her out nothing to eat. But " Daddy " was fond of the bright-eyed, warm-hearted lassie, and he always hid some bananas and other fruit and passed them to her in secret. There was no factory whistle to warn her in the morning, and sometimes she would start up in the middle of the night and, seeing her room almost as light as midday, would hastily put on her clothes, thinking she had slept in, and run out to ring the first bell, only to find a very quiet world and the great round moon shining in the sky.

It was not long before all the light and colour and beauty of the land seemed to fade away, and only the horror of a great darkness remain. She was taken to the homes and yards of the natives in the town and out into the bush, and saw a savage heathenism that astonished and shocked her. She did not think that people could be so wretched and degraded and ignorant. At some of the places the naked children were so afraid of her that they ran away screaming. She herself shrank from the fierce men who thronged round her, but her winning way captured their hearts, and she was soon quite at home with them.

When she came back she was very thoughtful, and talked to Mrs. Anderson of the things she had seen.

" My lassie," said " Mammy," " you've seen nothing." And she began to tell her of the terrible evils that filled the land with misery and sorrow.

" All around us, in the bush and far away into the

interior, there are millions of these black people. In every little village there is a Chief or Master, and a few free men and women, but the rest are slaves, and can be sold or flogged or killed at their owner's pleasure. It is all right when they are treated kindly, but think of the kind of men the masters are. All the tribes are wild and cruel and cunning, and pass their days and nights in fighting each other and in dancing and drinking, and there are some that are cannibals and feast on the bodies of those they have slain. Their religion is the fear of spirits, one of blood and sacrifice, in which there is no *love*. When a chief dies, do you know what happens to his wives and slaves? Their heads are cut off and they are buried with him to be his companions in the spirit-land."

Mary shivered. "It must be awful for the children," she said.

"Ah, yes, nearly all are slaves, and their masters look upon them as if they were sheep or pigs. They are his wealth. As soon as they are able to walk they begin to carry loads on their heads, and paddle canoes and sweep and clean out the yards. Often they are beaten or branded with a hot iron, or get their ears cut off. They sleep on the ground without any covering. When the girls grow up they are hidden away in the *ufōk nkukhō*, or 'house of seclusion,' and made very fat, and then become the slave-wives of the masters or freemen. And the twins! Poor mites. For some reason the people fear them worse than death, and they are not allowed to live; they are killed and crushed into pots and thrown away for leopards to eat. The mother is hounded into the bush, where she must live alone. She, too, is afraid of the twin-babies, and she would murder them if others did not."

Mary cried out in hot rage against so cruel a system. "Oh," she said, "I want to fight it; I want to save those innocent babes."

"Right, lassie," replied "Mammy," "and we need a hundred more like you to help."

Mary jumped to her feet. "The first thing I have to do," she said, "is to learn the language. I can do nothing until I know it well."

Efik is the chief tongue spoken in this part of Africa, and so quickly did she pick it up and master it that the people said she was "blessed with an Efik mouth"; and then her old dream came true, and she began to teach the black boys and girls in the day school. There were not many, for the chiefs did not believe in educating them. The bigger ones wore only a red or white shirt, while the wee ones had nothing on at all, and they carried their slates on their heads and their pencils in their woolly hair. In spite of everything they were a happy lot, with bright eyes and nimble feet, and Mary loved them, and those that were mischievous most of all. She also went down to the yards out of which they came, and spoke to their fathers and mothers about Jesus, and begged them to come to the Mission church.

When she had been out three years she fell ill, and was home-sick for her mother and friends. Calabar then was like some of the flowers growing in the bush, very pretty but very poisonous. Mary had fever so badly and was so weak that she was glad to be put on board the steamer and taken away.

In Scotland the cool winds and the loving care of her mother soon made her strong again.

Sometimes she was asked to speak at meetings, but was very shy to face people. One Sunday morning in Edinburgh she went to a children's church. The superintendent asked her to come to the platform, but she would not go. Then he explained to the children who she was and begged her to tell them something about Calabar. She blushed and refused. A hymn was given out, during which the superintendent pled with her to say a few words. "No, no, I cannot," she replied timidly. He was not to be beaten "Let us pray," he said. He prayed that Miss Slessor might be able to give them a message. When he finished he appealed to her again. After a pause she rose, and, turning her head half-away, spoke, not about Calabar, but about the free and glad life which children in a Christian land enjoyed, and how grateful they ought to be to Jesus, to whom they owed it all.

When she reached Calabar again she was made very happy, for her dream was to be a real missionary, and she found that she was to be in charge of the women's work at Old Town, a place two miles higher up the river, noted for its wickedness. She could now do as she liked, and save more money to send home to her mother and sisters, for they were always first in her thoughts. She lived in a hut built of mud and slips of bamboo, with a roof of palm leaves, wore old clothes and ate the cheap food of the natives, yam and plantain and fish. Many white persons wondered why she did this, and made remarks, but she did not tell them the reason: she cared less than ever for the laughter and scorn of others.

She soon became a power in the district. The men in the town were selfish and greedy, and would not let the inland natives come with their palm oil and trade with the factories, and fights often took place, and blood was shed. "This will never do," Mary said, and she began to help the country people, allowing them to steal down at night through the Mission ground, and guiding them past the sentries to the beach. The townsmen were angry, but they could not browbeat the brave white woman, and at last they gave in, and so the trading became free.

Then she began to oppose the custom of killing twins, and by and by she came to be known as "the Ma who loves babies." "Ma" in the Efik tongue is a title of respect given to women, and ever after she was known to all, white and black, as "Ma Slessor," or "Ma Akamba," the great Ma, or just simply "Ma," and we, too, may use the same name for her.

One day a young Scottish trader named Owen came to her with a black baby in his arms.

"Ma," he said, "I have found this baby thing lying away in the bush. It's a twin. The other has been killed. It would soon have died if I hadn't picked it up. I knew you'd like it, and so here it is."

Ma thanked the young man for his kindly act, and took the child, a bright and attractive girl, to her heart of hearts. "I'll call it Janie," she said, "after my sister."

She was delighted one day to hear that the British Consul and the missionaries had at last coaxed the chiefs in the river towns to make a law after their own fashion against twin-murder. This was done through a secret society called Egbo, which was very powerful and ruled the land. Those who belonged to it sent out men with whips and drums, called runners, who were disguised in masks and strange dresses. When they appeared all women and children had to fly indoors. If caught they were flogged. It was these men who came to proclaim the new rules. Ma thus tells about the scene in a letter to Sunday School children in Dundee :

Just as it became dark one evening I was sitting in my verandah talking to the children, when we heard the beating of drums and the singing of men coming near. This was strange, because we are on a piece of ground which no one in the town has a right to enter. Taking the wee twin boys in my hands I rushed out, and what do you think I saw? A crowd of men standing outside the fence chanting and swaying their bodies. They were proclaiming that all twins and twin-mothers could now live in the town, and that if any one murdered the twins or harmed the mothers he would be hanged by the neck. If you could have heard the twin-mothers who were there, how they laughed and clapped their hands and shouted, "Sosoño! Sosoño!" ("Thank you! Thank you!"). You will not wonder that amidst all the noise I turned aside and wept tears of joy and thankfulness, for it was a glorious day for Calabar.

A few days later the treaties were signed, and at the same time a new King was crowned. Twin-mothers were actually sitting with us on a platform in front of all the people. Such a thing had never been known before. What a scene it was! How can I describe it? There were thousands of Africans, each with a voice equal to ten men at home, and all speaking as loudly as they could. The women were the worst. I asked a chief to stop the noise. "Ma," he said, "how I fit stop them woman mouth?" The Consul told the King that he *must* have quiet during the reading of the treaties, but the King said helplessly, "How can I do? They be women—best put them away," and many *were* put away.

And the dresses! As some one said of a hat I trimmed, they were "overpowering." The women had crimson silks and satins covered with ear-rings and brooches and all kinds of finery. The men were in all sorts of uniform with gold and silver lace and jewelled hats and caps. Many naked bodies were covered with beadwork, silks, damask, and even red and green table-cloths trimmed with gold and silver. Their legs were circled with brass and beadwork, and unseen bells that tinkled all the time. The hats were immense affairs with huge feathers of all colours and brooches.

The Egbo men were the most gorgeous. Some had large three-cornered hats with long plumes hanging down. Some had crowns, others wore masks of animals with horns, and all were looped round with ever so many skirts and trailed tails a yard or two long with a tuft of feathers at the end.

Such splendour is barbaric, but it is imposing in its own place.

Well, the people have agreed to do away with many of the bad customs they have that hinder the spread of the Gospel. You must remember that it is the long and faithful teaching of God's word that is bringing the people to a state of mind fit for better things.

Now I am sleepy. Good-bye. May God make us all worthy of what He has done for us.

The people were good for a time, but soon fell back into the habit of centuries, and did in secret what they used to do openly. Ma saw that the struggle was only just beginning, and she threw herself into it with all her courage and strength.

She was always studying her Bible, and learning more of the love and power of Jesus, and so much did she lean on Him that she was growing quite fearless, and would go by herself into the vilest haunts in the town or far out into lonesome villages. Often she took a canoe and went up the river and into the creeks and visited places where no white woman had been before, healing the sick, sitting by the wayside listening to the tales of the people, and talking to them about the Saviour of the world. Sometimes there was so much to say and do that she could not get back the same day, and she slept on straw or leaves in the open air or on a bundle of rags in an evil-smelling hut.

Once she took the house-children and went a long river journey to visit an exiled chief who lived in a district haunted by elephants. They were to start in the morning, but things are done very leisurely in Africa, and it was night before they set off by torchlight. Eyo Honesty VII, the negro king of Creek Town, who was a Christian and always very kind to Ma, had sent a State canoe, brightly painted, with the message:

"Ma must not go as a nameless stranger to a strange people, but as a lady and our Mother, and she can use the canoe as long as she pleases."

There was a crew of thirty-three men dressed only in loin-cloths.

As they dipped the paddles and sped onwards over the quiet water, a drummer drummed his drum, and the crew chanted a song in her praise:

Ma, our beautiful beloved mother is on board,
Ho, ho, ho!

The motion of the canoe was like a cradle, and the song like a mother's crooning, and she fell asleep; and all through the night, amongst these wild black men, she lay in God's keeping like a little child.

At dawn they came to a beach and a village, where she was given a mud room in the chief's yard, and here for a whole fortnight she lived in the company of dogs, fowls, rats, lizards, and mosquitoes. Many of the people had never seen a white person, and were afraid to touch her. She was very sorry for them, they were so poor and naked and dirty, and she busied herself making clothes and healing the sick. So many were ill that a canoe had to be sent to the nearest Mission House for another supply of medicines.

One day the chief said to her, "Ma, two of my wives have been doing wrong, and they are to get one hundred stripes each on their bare backs. It is the custom."

She was horrified. "Why, what have they done?"

"They went into a yard that is not their own. Of course," he added, "they are young and thoughtless, they are only sixteen years old, but they must learn."

"Oh, but that is a very cruel punishment for young girls."

"Ma, it is nothing; we shall also rub salt into the wounds and perhaps cut off their ears. That is the only way to make the women obey us."

"No, no, you must not do that," cried Ma. "Bring all the people together for a palaver."

The crowd gathered, and the two girls stood in front with sullen faces. Ma spoke to them.

"You have done wrong according to your law and you will have to be punished."

At this, smiles broke over the faces of the men; but Ma turned to them swiftly and cried: "You are in the wrong too. Shame on you for making a law that marries girls so early! Why, these are still children who love fun and mischief. Their fault is a small one, and you must not punish them so cruelly."

The smiles fled, and the faces grew angry and defiant, and there were mutterings and threats.

"Who are you to come and spoil our laws," said some of the big men ; "the girls are ours, let us have them."

But Ma was firm, and as she was the guest of the village, and worthy of honour, they at length agreed to give a lighter punishment. The girls were handed over to two strong fellows, who flogged them with a whip. Ma heard their screams amidst the shouts and laughter of those who looked on, and was ready to attend to their bleeding bodies when they ran into her room. Then she gave them something which made them sleep and forget their pain and misery.

"What can you expect ?" said she to herself ; "they have never heard of God, they worship human skulls, and they don't know about love and compassion and mercy"—and she did her best to teach them.

In the quiet nights, when their work in the fields was over, they came and squatted on the ground, the big men in front, the slaves outside, and she stood beside a little table on which were a Bible and hymn-book and a lamp, and in her sweet and earnest voice told them the story of the gentle Jesus. She could not see anything but the dark mass of their bodies and the gleaming of their eyes, and they sat so still that when she stopped she could only hear the sighing of the wind among the palm tops. It was all very wonderful to them. Sometimes they would ask questions, chiefly about the life after death, which was such a mystery to them, and, when they rose, they slipped away softly to their homes to talk about this strange new religion that was so different from their own.

It was the time of storms, and one day when Ma was sitting sewing the sky grew dark, lightning flashed, thunder crashed, and floods fell. The roof of the hut was blown away, and she was drenched to the skin, and for a time was ill with fever and nigh to death.

On the way back at night to Old Town another tornado burst, flooding the canoe, and tossing it about like a match-box on the raging waves. The crew lost their wits, and Ma thought they would be upset. But putting aside her own fear for the sake of others, she made the men paddle into the mangrove, where they jumped into the branches like monkeys and held on to the canoe until the danger was passed. All were sitting in water, and Ma was wet through and shaking with ague. She became so ill that when Old Town was reached she had to be carried up to the Mission House. Yet she did not go to bed until she had made hot tea for the children, and tucked them snugly away for the night.

Soon afterwards another tornado destroyed her house and she and the children escaped through the wind and rain to the home of some white traders who were very kind to her. But she was so ill after all she had gone through that she was ordered to Scotland, and had again to be carried on board the steamer. She would not leave Janie behind her, as she was afraid the people would murder her, and so the girl-twin also sailed with her across the sea.

Ma soon grew strong in her native air, and one Sunday she went to her old church in Dundee with Janie, and there in the Sunday School, the black child was baptised and given the name that had been chosen for her. With her black skin and her solemn eyes she was a curious sight to the boys and girls, and they came crowding round and begged to be allowed to hold her for a little. She appeared at many of the meetings to which Ma went, and during the address would sit on the platform munching biscuits, which she was always ready to share with every one near her.

One night Ma travelled to Falkirk to speak to a large class of girls taught by Miss Bessie Wilson, a well-known lady in the Church. She had a message that night, and her face shone and her words fell like stirring music on the young hearts before her. Janie was passed round from one to another, and helped to make her story more real. So delighted were the girls with the black baby that they begged to be allowed to give something every month for her support.

Perhaps all this had nothing to do with what happened afterwards, but was it not strange that out of that class by and by no fewer than six members gave themselves to the work in Calabar, including Miss Wright and Miss Peacock, two of Ma's dearest friends and best helpers?

Ma had a wonderful power of drawing other people to her and of influencing them for good. On this visit one girl, Miss Hogg, was no sooner in her company than she decided to go to Calabar, and she went, and was for many years a much-loved missionary, whose name was familiar to the children of the Church at home.

Ma was anxious to be back at her work, but her sister Janie, who was delicate like her brothers, needed all her care, and was at last ordered by the doctor to live in a warmer climate. This set Ma dreaming again. "If only I could take her out to Calabar with me," she mused, "we could live cheaply in a native hut, and it might save her life." But the Mission Board did not think this would be right, and Mary, who had a quick brain as well as a warm heart, at once carried Janie off to Devonshire, that lovely county in the south of England, where she rented a house with a garden and nursed and cared for the invalid. Very sorrowfully she gave up the work in Calabar she loved so much, but she felt that her sister needed her most. Then she brought down her mother, and they lived happily together, and Janie grew strong in the sunshine and fresh air. After a time Ma thought they could be left, and after getting an old companion down from Dundee to look after them, she went out again to Africa.

Her new station was Creek Town, a little farther away, where the missionary was her dear friend Mr. Goldie, the *etubom akamba*, the "big master." Here she lived more plainly than ever, for she needed now to send a larger sum of money in order to keep the home in Devonshire. But she had not long to do this loving service, for first her mother, and then her sister, died. All the rest of the family of seven had now passed away, and Ma was alone in the world. She never quite got over her grief and her longing for them all, and to the end of her life was dreaming a sweet dream of the time when she would meet them again in heaven.

With no home-hearts to love she began to lavish her affection on the black children, and was specially fond of Janie, who trotted at her side all day and slept in her bed at night. She was a lively thing, full of fun and tricks, and it was curious that the people should be so afraid of her. They would not touch her even if Ma was there.

One day a man came to the Mission House who said he was her father.

"Then," said Ma, "you will come and see her."

"Oh, no," he replied, with fear in his eyes, "I could not."

Ma looked at him with scorn. "What harm can a wee girlie do you?" she asked. "Come along."

"Well, I'll look from a distance."

"Hoots," she cried, and seizing him by the arm dragged him close to the child, who was alarmed and clung to Ma. "My lassie, this is your father, give him a hug."

The child put her arms round the man's neck and he did not mind, and indeed his fierce face grew soft, and he sat down and took her gently on his knee and petted her, and was so delighted with her pretty ways that he would hardly give her up. After that he came often and brought her gifts of food. Thus Ma tried to show the people that there was nothing wrong with twins, and that it was a cruel and senseless thing to kill them.

There were other children, both boys and girls, in the home, whom Ma had saved from sickness or death, and these she trained to do housework and bake and go to market, and when their work was done she taught them from their Efik lesson books, and by and by they were able to help her in school and church by looking after all the little things that needed to be done. The oldest was a girl of thirteen, a kind of Cinderella, who was always in the kitchen, but who was very honest and truthful and loved her Ma.

Besides these there were always a number of refugees in the yard-rooms outside, a woman, perhaps, who had been ill-used by her masters and had run away, or girls broken in body and mind, who had been brought down from the country to be sold as slaves and whom Ma had rescued, or sick people who came from far distances to get the white woman's medicine to be healed.

It was a busy life which Ma lived in and out amongst the huts and villages of the Creek; but she was happy, like all busy people who love their work and are doing good.

CHAPTER III

Ma's great adventure: how she went up-river by herself in a canoe and lived in a forest amongst a savage tribe; how she fought their terrible customs and saved many lives; how she built a hut for herself and then a church, and how she took a band of the wild warriors down to the coast and got them to be friends with the people who had always been their sworn enemies.

MA felt that she was not getting to the heart of things.

Behind that wall of bush, for hundreds of miles inland, lay a vast region of forest and river into which white men had not yet ventured. It was there that the natives lived almost like wild beasts, and where the most terrible crimes against women and children were done without any one lifting a finger to stop them. It was there that the biggest work for Jesus was to be carried on. "If only I could get amongst these people," she said, "and attack their customs at the root; that is where they must be destroyed."

She dreamed of it night and day, and laid her plans.

One district lying between two rivers behind Creek Town, called Okoyong, was specially noted for its lawless heathenism. The tribe who lived there was strong, proud, warlike, and had become the terror of the whole country. Every man, woman, and child of them went about armed, and even ate and slept with their guns and swords by their side; they roamed about in bands watching the forest paths, and attacked and captured all whom they met, and sold them as slaves or sent them away to be food for the cannibals. They and the people of the coast were sworn enemies.

Ma knew all about them, and was eager to go into their midst to teach them better ways. She pled with the Mission leaders at Duke Town. "I am not afraid," she said; "I am alone now and have nobody to be anxious about me."

But the missionaries shook their heads. "No, no, it is too dangerous," they told her.

And her friends the traders said, "It is a gunboat they want, Ma, not a missionary."

It was hard for her eager spirit to wait. For fourteen

years she had worked in the factory at Dundee, for ten more she had toiled in the towns on the Calabar River, and she was now a grown woman. But God often keeps us at a task far longer than we ourselves think is good for us, for He knows best, and if we are patient to the end He lets us do even more than we had hoped for. So it was with Mary Slessor. She was at last allowed to go.

The Okoyong people, however, would not have her.

"We want no missionary, man or woman," they said sullenly.

For a whole year messengers went up and down the river, but the tribe remained firm. Then Ma said:

"I'll go myself and see them."

One hot June day she got the loan of King Eyo's canoe, a hollow tree-trunk twenty feet long, on which there was a little arch of palm leaves to shade her from the sun, and set out up the Calabar River. As she lay back on a pillow she thought how pretty and peaceful the scene was—the calm water gleaming in the light of the sky, the cotton trees and bananas and palms along the banks, the brilliant birds and butterflies flitting about. The only sound was the dip of the paddles and the soft voices of the men singing about their Ma. And then she thought of what might lie before her, of the perils of the forest, and the anger of the bloodthirsty Okoyong, and wondered if she had done right.

"We'll have a cup of tea, anyhow," she said to herself, and got out an old paraffin stove, but found that matches had been forgotten. Coming to a farm the canoe swung into a mud-beach, and Ma went ashore, and was happy to find that the owner was a "big" man whom she knew. He gave her some matches, and on they went again. When the tea was ready Ma opened a tin of stewed steak and cut up a loaf of home-made bread.

"Boy," she said, "where is the cup?"

"No cup, Ma—forgotten."

"Bother! now what shall I do?"

"I wash out that steak tin, Ma."

"Right; if you use what you have you will never want."

But alas! the tin slipped out of his hand and sank.

Ma was a philosopher. "Ah, well," she said, "it cannot be helped. I'll drink out of the saucer."

Ma was really very timid. Just before leaving Devonshire she would not go out on Guy Fawkes' Day, because she shrank from the crowds who were parading the streets; and yet, here she was going alone into an unknown region in Africa to face untamed savages. What made her so courageous was her faith in God. She believed that He wanted her to do this bit of work, and that therefore He would take care of her. She would not carry a weapon of any kind. Even David, when he went out to fight Goliath, had a sling and a stone as well as his faith. Ma was going to fight a much bigger giant, and she took nothing with her but a bright face and a heart full of love and sympathy. She was more like Jesus, who faced His enemies with nothing but the power of His spirit.

The paddlers landed her at a strip of beach on the river, and with a fast-beating heart she trudged along the forest path for about four miles until she reached a village called Ekenge.

Shouts arose: "Ma has come! Ma has come!" and a crowd rushed forward. To her surprise they seemed pleased to see her. "You are brave to come alone," they said; "that is good."

The chief, who was called Edem, was sober, and he would not allow her to go on farther, because the people at the next village were drunk and might harm her. So she stayed the night at Ekenge.

"I am not very particular about my bed nowadays," she told a friend, "but as I lay on a few dirty sticks laid across and across and covered with a litter of dirty cornshells, with plenty of rats and insects, three women and an infant three days old alongside, and over a dozen goats and sheep and cows and countless dogs outside, you don't wonder that I slept little! But I had such a comfortable quiet night in my own heart."

Next day all the big men of the district came to see her, and her winsome ways won them over, and they agreed to give her ground for a church and school, and promised that when these were built they would be places of refuge into which hunted people could fly and be safe.

She was so happy that she did not mind the rain, which came on and wetted her to the skin as she walked back through the forest to the river. The tide, too, was against the paddlers, so they had to put the canoe into a cove and tie it to a tree for two hours. Ma was cold and shivery, and lay watching the brown crabs fighting in the mud, but she dared not sleep in case a crocodile or snake might make an attack. The men kept very quiet, and sometimes she heard them whisper, " Speak softly and let Ma sleep," or " Don't shake the canoe and wake Ma." When they started again she gradually passed into sleep, and only wakened to see the friendly lamps of Creek Town gleaming like stars through the night.

A month or two later she was ready to go and make her home among the Okoyong. The people of Creek Town were alarmed, and tried to make her give up the idea.

" Do you think any one will listen to you ? "

" Do you think they will lay aside their weapons of war for you ? "

" We shall never see you again."

" You are sure to be murdered."

Such were some of the things said to her. But she just smiled, and thought how little there was to fear when Jesus was with her.

" I am going," she wrote home, " to a new tribe up-country, a fierce, cruel people, and every one tells me they will kill me. But I don't fear any hurt. Only—to combat their savage customs will require courage and firmness on my part."

The night before she left she could not sleep for thinking and wondering about all that was before her, and lay listening to the dripping of the rain until daylight. When she heard the negro carriers coming for the packages she rose. It was still wet, and the men were miserable and grumbled and quarrelled amongst themselves until good King Eyo arrived and took them in hand. Seeing how nervous she was he sat down beside her and cheered her up, saying that he would send secret messengers from time to time to find out how she was getting on, and that she was to let him know if ever she needed help. Her courage and smiles came back, and she jumped up, gathered her children together, and walked down to the beach. Amidst the sighs and sobs and farewells of the people she stepped into the canoe.

"Good-bye, good-bye," she cried to every one, and the canoe sped into the middle of the stream and was lost in the mist and the rain.

It was night when the landing-beach was reached, and the stars were hidden by rain-clouds. As Ma stepped ashore on the mud-bank and looked into the dark forest and thought of the long journey before her, and the end of it, her heart failed. She might lose her way in that unlit tangle of wood. She would meet wild beasts, the natives might be feasting and drinking and unwilling to receive her. A score of shadowy terrors arose in her imagination. For a moment she wished she could turn back to the safe shelter of her home, but when she thought of Jesus and what He had done for her sake, how He was never afraid, but went forward calm and fearless even to His death on the Cross, she felt ashamed of her weakness, and, calling the children, she plunged stoutly into the black depths of the forest.

What a queer procession it was! The biggest boy, eleven years old, went first with a box of bread and tea and sugar on his head, next a laddie of eight with a kettle and pots, then a wee fellow of three sturdily doing his best, but crying as if his heart would break. Janie followed, also sobbing, and lastly the white mother herself carrying Annie, a baby slave-girl, on her shoulder, and singing gaily to cheer the others, but there was often a funny little break in her voice as she heard the scream of the vampire-bat or the stealthy tread and growling of wild animals close at hand.

Brushing against dripping branches, stumbling in the black and slippery mud, tired and hungry and wretched, they made their way to Ekenge. When they arrived all was quiet, and no one greeted them.

"Strange," said Ma to herself, for a village welcome is always a noisy one. She shouted, and two slaves appeared.

"Where is the chief? Where are the people?" she asked.

"Gone to the death-feast at Ifako, the next village, Ma."

"Then bring me some fire and water."

She made tea for the children, undressed them, huddled them naked in a corner to sleep, and sat down in her wet things to wait for the carriers, who were bringing the boxes with food and dry clothes. A messenger arrived, but it was to tell her that the men were too worn out to carry anything that night. She jumped to her feet, and, bare-headed and barefooted, dived into the forest to return to the river. She had not gone far when she heard the pitter-patter of feet. She stopped.

"Ma! Ma!" a voice cried. It was the messenger. He loved Ma, and, unhappy at the thought of her tramping along that lonesome trail, he had followed her to keep her company. Together they ran, now tripping and falling, now dashing into a tree, now standing still trembling, as they heard some rushing sound or weird cry.

When she came to the beach she waded out to the canoe, lifted the covering, and roused the sleeping natives. They grumbled a good deal, but even these big rough men could not withstand Ma's coaxing, masterful ways, and they had soon the boxes on their heads and were marching merrily in single file along the wet and dark path to Ekenge. She made them put the packages into the hut which Edem, the chief, had allotted to her: a small dirty place with mud walls, no window, and only an open space for a door. When everything was piled up inside there was hardly room for herself and the children, but she lay down on the boxes, and as it was after midnight, and she was weary and footsore, she soon fell into a deep sleep.

When the chief and his followers came back from the revels at Ifako they welcomed Ma, for it was an honour for a white woman to live in their midst. But they had no idea of changing their ways of life for her, and went on day and night drinking rum and gin, dancing, and making sacrifices to their jujus or gods. Sometimes the din was so great that Ma never got a wink of sleep. The yard was full of half-naked slave-women, who were always scolding and quarrelling. Some were wicked and hateful, and did not want such a good white Ma to be with them, and tried to force her to leave. But there was one who was kind to her, Eme Ete, a sister of the chief, who had a sad story. One day she told it to Ma. She had been married to a chief who had not treated her well. When he died his followers put the blame on his wives, and they were seized and brought to trial. It was an odd way they had of testing guilt or innocence. As each wife stepped forward the head of a fowl was cut off, and the people watched to see how the body fell. If it lay in a certain way she was innocent; if in another way, she was guilty! How Eme Ete trembled when her turn came! When she knew she was safe she fainted.

Eme Ete was big in body and big in heart. To Ma she showed herself gentle and refined, and acted towards her as a white lady would, caring for her comfort, watching over her safety, going to her meetings, and helping her in her work. They grew to be like sisters. Yet Eme Ete was always a little bit of a mystery to Ma. She wanted the people to change their old ways, but she herself would not, and went on with her bush-worship and sacrifices, and never became a Christian. But of all the native women Ma ever met, there was none she loved so well as this motherly heathen soul.

In the yard there were also many boys and girls. Ma was fond of children, but these ones were not nice: they stole and lied and made themselves a trouble to everybody. "Oh, dear," she sighed, "what can I do with such bairns?" But she remembered what her Master said, "Suffer little children to come unto Me and forbid them not"; and she gathered them about her, took the wee ones in her arms and nursed them, made clothes for their bodies, and taught them what it was to be clean and sweet and good. When the sick babies died she would not let the people throw them away into the bush, as they usually did, but put them into little boxes on which she laid some flowers, and buried them in a piece of ground that she chose for a cemetery. "Why, Ma," said the natives in wonder, "what is a dead child? You can have hundreds of them."

None of the children could read or write, nor, indeed, could any of the older people, and so Ma started schools, which she held in the open air in the shade of the forest trees. At first everybody came, even the grey-headed men and women, and learned A B C in Efik and sang the hymns that Ma taught them. The beautiful birds which flew above their heads must have wondered, for they had only been accustomed to the wild chant of war-songs. And at night the twinkling stars must have twinkled harder when they looked down and saw, not a crowd of people drinking and fighting, but a quiet company, and a white woman standing talking to them in grave sweet tones about holy things.

But when Ma spoke about their bad customs they would not listen. "Ma," they would say, "we like you and we want to learn book and wear clothes, but we don't want to put away our old fashions."

"Well," replied Ma patiently, "we shall see."

And so the battle began.

The first time she failed, because she did not know what was happening. A lad had been accused of some fault, and she saw him standing, girt with chains, holding out his arms before a pot of boiling oil. A man took a ladle and dipped it into the burning stuff, which he began to pour over the boy's hands. Ma sprang forward, but was too late; the boy screamed and rolled on the ground in agony. She was very angry, especially when they told her the meaning of the thing. It was a test to show whether the boy was innocent or guilty of the charge brought against him. If he had not been guilty, they said, he would not have suffered.

"Oh, you stupid creatures," cried Ma. "Everybody will suffer if you do that to them. Let me try it on you," she said to the man with the ladle, but he rushed off amidst the laughter of the crowd.

Next time she did better. A slave was blamed for using witchcraft, and condemned to die. Ma knew he was innocent, and went and stood beside him in front of the armed warriors of the chief, and said:

"This man has done no wrong. You must not put him to death."

"Ho, ho," they cried, "that is not good speaking. We have said he shall die, and he must die."

"No, no; listen," and she tried to reason with them, but they came round her waving their swords and guns, and shouting at the pitch of their voices. She stood in the midst of them as she had stood in the midst of the Dundee roughs, pale, but calm and unafraid. The more angry and excited and threatening they grew the cooler she became. Perhaps it was her wonderful courage which did not fail her even when the swords were flashing about her head, perhaps it was the strange light that shone in her face that awed and quietened them, but the confusion died down and ceased. Then the chiefs agreed for her sake not to kill the man, but they put heavy chains upon his arms and legs, and starved and flogged him until he was a mass of bleeding flesh. Ma felt she had not done much, but it was a beginning.

People at a distance heard of her, and one day messengers came from a township many miles away to ask her to visit their chief, who was believed to be dying.

"And what will happen if he dies?" asked Ma.

"All his wives and slaves will be killed," was the prompt reply.

"Then I will come at once," she said.

"Ma," put in Chief Edem, "you must not go. They are cruel people and may do you hurt. Then see the rain; all the rivers will be flowing and you cannot cross."

But Ma thought of the women who might be murdered, and she went. The rain poured down, and as she fought her way for eight hours through the forest her clothes became soaked and torn, and she threw most of them off and left them. As she trudged with bare head and bare feet through the villages on the way, she looked very ragged and forlorn, and the people gazed at her in wonder. When she reached the township she found the men armed and ready to begin the slaughter, and the women sad and afraid. Although she was wet and cold and feverish, she went straight to the hut of the sick chief and nursed him, and gradually brought him back to health, so that there was no more thought of sacrifice and blood.

Her next trouble was in her own yard. Edem, her chief, was kind to her, but he was also under the power of the old bad ideas and believed in the witch-doctors, cunning fellows who pretended to know the cause of sickness and how to cure it. Falling ill he called in one of these medicine-men, who declared that an enemy had placed a number of things in his body, and made believe to take them out. When Ma came Edem held them up—cartridges, powder, teeth, bones, eggshells, and seeds—and said: "Ma, a dreadful battle has been going on during the night. See what wicked persons have done to me." Her heart sank: she knew what would follow.

Sure enough a number of men and women were seized and chained to posts and condemned to die. Ma set herself to save them. She begged and coaxed the sick man so much on their behalf that at last she wearied him, and he got his followers to carry him secretly away to one of his farms. Ma could only pray, and she prayed that he might get better. By and by strength did return, and the prisoners were released, only one woman being put to death.

No sooner was this trial ended than a worse came. A chief whom Ma feared, a very cruel and bloodthirsty man, paid a visit to Edem. He and his followers did nothing but drink, and soon they were mad with the fiery liquor, and the whole village was in a violent uproar. Ma bravely went into the midst of the mob and sought to calm them. She saw that the best thing to do was to get the visitors away, and she hurried them off as quickly as possible, going with them herself in order to prevent bloodshed on the way, for they wanted to fight every one they met. In the forest path they saw some withered plants and leaves on the ground. "Sorcery," they yelled, and fled back in a panic—they thought these things had magic in them and were meant to do them harm.

"Let us go to the last village and kill every one in it," they shouted; "they have tried to bewitch us."

And they rushed pell-mell along the path flourishing their swords and shouting their terrible war-cries. Ma prayed for swiftness, and ran until she came in front of them, and then turning, she threw out her arms and breathlessly dared them to pass. It seemed a mad thing to do, but again that something in her face made them stop. They argued with her and then they obeyed her, and went forward by another path. But they began to dance and caper and fight each other, until Ma, with the help of some of the soberer ones, tied the worst to the trees. The others went on, and she did not leave them until they were safe in their own district. On the way back she unloosed the drunken prisoners, who were now in a raging temper, and sent them home with their hands fastened behind their backs.

But that was not the end. Next day the cruel chief went to the village that was blamed for laying the things on the path, and although it did not belong to him, but to Edem, he made the people take ordeals, and carried away a young man in handcuffs to put him to death. Ma hastened to the chief. He was rude and rough, and laughed at her, but she tried not to mind, and begged hard for the lad's life. When she returned she found that Edem was getting ready to fight, and she prayed earnestly that the heart of the cruel chief might be softened. It was softened, for news came that the prisoner had been sent home, and so there was peace and not war.

Ma began to wonder how long she would be able to live in the midst of such sin and dirt. She had hung a door at the opening of her mud-room, and made a hole in the wall for a window and curtained it with pieces of cloth, but the place was so small that at night she had to lift her boxes outside in order to give herself and the children room to sleep. It was overrun with rats and lizards and beetles and all sorts of biting insects. She could not get away from the squabbling and bad language and rioting of the wives and slaves, and was often tired and ill. It was the thought of Jesus that gave her patience and courage. She remembered how He had left His home above the stars and dwelt on earth amongst men who were unlovely and wicked and cruel, and how He never grumbled or gave in, though life to Him was often bitter and hard. "Shall I not follow my Master," she said, "because my way is not easy and not nice? Yes, I will be His true disciple and be strong and brave."

She was longing to be alone sometimes to read her Bible and think and pray in quiet, and one day she started to build a little hut of her own some distance away from the others. First she fixed stout tree-trunks in the ground, and on the tops of these, cross-wise, she laid other pieces. Sticks were then placed between the uprights, and strips of bamboo, beaten until soft, were fastened in and out, just as the threads had been woven in the loom of the Dundee factory. This was the skeleton of the hut, and when Ma looked at it she clapped her hands with delight.

"It's like playing a game," she said to the children.

The walls were next made by throwing in large lumps of red clay between the sticks. When the clay was dry the surface was rubbed smooth, and then mats of palm leaves were laid on the top and tied down to form the roof.

"Now for the furniture," she said. With kneaded lumps of clay she built up a fireplace, and moulded a seat beside it where the cook could sit, then made a sideboard, in which holes were scooped out for cups and bowls and plates, and a long couch, which she meant for herself. All these were beaten hard and polished and darkened with a native dye.

The flitting was great fun to the children. So many of the pots and pans and jars were hung on bits of wood on the posts outside that Ma declared the house was like one of the travelling caravans she used to see in Scotland ; and so she called it " The Caravan." When everything was finished she stood and looked at it with a twinkle in her eye. " Be it ever so humble," she said gaily, " there's no place like home ! " Then they sat down to a merry meal. What did it matter if there was only one dish and no spoons or forks ? There was no happier family in all the land that night.

Ma was now able to read her Bible in peace and pray to God in quietness and comfort. But outside she had still the goats and fowls and rats and the insects and even the wild things of the forest, and sometimes they came in. One morning when she awoke, she saw on her bed a curious thing, and found that it was the skin of a snake that had stolen in during the night and shed its old clothes as these reptiles sometimes do. So she began to dream of a bigger house with an upstairs, where she could be safer.

But first there must be a church. The chief and free men and women helped, and by and by there rose a long roomy shed, complete, except for a door and windows. What a day it was when it was set apart and used for the worship of God—the first church in wild Okoyong !

Ma told the people that they could not come to God's house except with clean bodies and clean hearts. Few of them had clean clothes, or clothes at all, and the children never wore any. But Ma had been receiving boxes from Sunday Schools and work-parties in Scotland, and out of these she dressed the women and little ones in pinafores of all colours. How proud and happy they were ! But the excitement died into quietness and reverence when they went inside the building, and an awe fell upon them as Ma explained what a church meant, and that God was in their midst.

The chiefs rose and said that they would respect the building, that no weapon of war would ever be brought into it, and that all their quarrels would be left outside; and they promised to send their followers to the services and their children to the schools.

But like some better people at home these wayward savages could not be good for long. They went back to their evil doings, and were soon away raiding and fighting, leaving only a few women and the children in the village. It was the rum and gin that caused most of the mischief. Every one drank, and often Ma went to bed knowing that there was not one sober person for miles around. The horrible stuff came up from the coast, having been shipped overseas from Christian countries. Ma never ceased to wonder how white men could seek to ruin native people for the sake of money. It made her very angry, and she fought the trade with all her power.

"Do you know," she said one day to her chief, "you drink because you have not enough work. We have a rhyme in our country which says:

Satan finds some mischief still
For idle hands to do.

Why don't you trade with Calabar?"

He grinned. "We do trade with Calabar," he said; "we trade in heads."

"Well, you must trade in palm oil and food instead. And first you must make peace."

"We can't do that, Ma, because Calabar won't come to Okoyong."

"Of course not, because they are afraid, and rightly too. Well, if they won't come to you, you must go to them."

"But, Ma, we would never come back."

"Tuts! I will go with you."

She made them go to the river and get a large canoe and fill it with yams and plantains (these were gifts for the Calabar people), and with bags of palm nuts and a barrel of oil (these were to begin trading with). But they knew little about boats, and they loaded it so high that it sank. Another was got, and all was ready, when some of the chiefs drew back and said they would only go if Ma allowed them to take their guns and swords.

"No, no," she said, "that would be foolish. We are going in peace and not in war."

"Ma, you make women of us! No man goes to a strange place without arms."

But she would not yield, and they started. Suddenly she caught sight of some swords hidden under the bags of nuts, and stooping, she seized them and pitched them out on the bank. "Go on," she cried, and the canoe swept down the river.

King Eyo received the trembling chiefs like a Christian gentleman, spoke to them kindly, and showed them over his large house. There was a palaver, and all quarrels between the two peoples were made up, and all evil thoughts of one another vanished, and the men from Okoyong went back astonished and joyful. They began to trade with the coast, and so busy did they become in their fields growing food and making palm oil that they had less time for drinking and fighting, and grew more sober and prosperous. They were very grateful to Ma.

"We are not treating her well," they said to one another. "We must build her a better house."

And they began to erect a large one with upstairs rooms and a verandah, but they could not manage the woodwork. Ma begged the Mission authorities to send up a carpenter to put in the doors and windows, and by and by one came from Scotland named Mr. Ovens, and appeared at Ekenge with his tools and Tom, a native apprentice, and set to work. Mr. Ovens was bright and cheery, and had a laugh that made everybody else want to laugh; and he made so light of the hard life he had to live that Ma praised God for sending him. Like herself, he spoke the dear Scots tongue and at night he sang the plaintive songs of their native land until she was ready to echo the words of Tom: "Master, I don't like these songs, they make my heart big and my eyes water."

CHAPTER IV

Stories of how Ma kept an armed mob at bay and saved the lives of a number of men and women; how in answer to a secret warning she tramped a long distance in the dark to stop a war; how she slept by a camp-fire in the heart of the forest, and how she became a British Consul and ruled Okoyong like a Queen.

A LOW wailing cry, with a note of terror in it, drifted out of the forest into the sunshine of the clearing where Ma was sitting watching the work on the new house. She leapt to her feet, and listened with a far-away look on her face. Next moment she sprang in amongst the trees and disappeared.

Mr. Ovens saw that the natives about him were uneasy, and when a messenger came running up and said, "You have to go to Ma and take medicine for an accident," they burst into loud lamentations. On reaching the spot he found that Etim, the son of the chief, a lad about twenty years of age, had been caught by a log which he had been handling, and struck senseless to the ground.

"This is not good for us," Ma said, shaking her head. "The people believe that accidents are caused by witchcraft, the witch-doctor will be called in to smell out the guilty ones, and many will suffer."

They carried the lad home, and she nursed him day and night, but life ebbed away; and one Sunday morning when all was quiet and beautiful, she heard again that strange wailing sound which told of peril and death. She rushed to the scene. The men were blowing smoke from a lighted palm leaf into the lad's nose, rubbing pepper into his eyes, and shouting into his ears to keep back the spirit.

"Silly babies," she could not help saying to herself.

"He is dead," cried the chief, and giving the body to Ma he shouted in a terrible voice:

"He has been killed by sorcerers, and they must die! Where is the witch-doctor?"

The witch-doctor came, an evil-looking man with cunning eyes, and after humming and hawing he blamed the people in a village near the spot where the accident happened.

"Off! seize them!" called the chief to his freemen.

But a swift foot had secretly carried a warning to the

village, and Chief Akpo and his followers had fled. Only a dozen men, and some women and babies who could not run, were captured, and they were loaded with chains and brought to Ekenge and imprisoned in a yard.

Ma felt that this was a big affair, and perhaps the turning-point in her life amongst the Okoyong.

"If these people are killed," she said, "all my work will be undone. I must prevent it at any cost."

And first she went away by herself and knelt down and prayed, and then came back calm and strong.

She knew what the natives liked, and hoping to please and soften Edem, she said to him, "I am going to honour your son." From her boxes she brought out fine silk cloth of many colours, shirts and vests and other clothes, and put them on the dead body. The head was shaved and painted yellow, and upon it was wound a turban, and above that a black and scarlet hat with plumes of feathers, and an umbrella. To one hand was tied a stick, and to the other a whip. Last of all a mirror was placed in front of the dead eyes, because the people believed the spirit would see what had been done and be glad. There he sat, the lifeless boy, with all his finery, a sad queer sight. When the people came in they yelled with delight, and danced and called for rum to make merry. Barrel after barrel was brought and emptied, and they began to grow wild, leaping about with swords and guns, and singing their weird tribal songs.

"Humph!" said Ma, "my cure seems to be as bad as the disease. Still, they have forgotten the prisoners."

These were chained to posts, and expected every minute to have their heads chopped off. They were all very miserable. The babies were crying, and there was a girl of fifteen who clung weeping to her mother, and ran up to any one who came, saying piteously, "Oh, I'll be a slave for life if only you will spare my mother."

Ma turned to Mr. Ovens. "We must not leave these poor creatures. You will watch by day, and I will watch by night, and we may save them yet."

So time and time about these two sat on guard. They had no weapons, they were alone in the midst of a drunken mob, and yet they had no fear, for they trusted God and believed that He would take care of them.

Because they were there, Edem and his brother chiefs did not touch the prisoners. Some days passed. Then one afternoon Ma saw little brown objects lying on a stone. ' Eseré beans ! " she exclaimed in alarm. These beans grow on a wild vine, and are very poisonous. She knew they were to be crushed and put in water, and given to the prisoners with the idea of finding out who was guilty of the death of Etim. Of course all who drank the water would die, and the people would believe that justice had been done. That was the only kind of justice they knew.

Ma sought out the chiefs and told them they must not do this wicked thing, and when they put her aside she followed them about and begged and worried them until they became angry.

" Let us alone," they cried. " What does it matter ? Your God will not let the innocent die."

Their followers grew excited, and some of them lost control of themselves and hustled Ma and threatened her.

" Make the dead live," they snarled, " and we shall give you the prisoners."

Ma's reply was to sit down and look at them with stern eyes.

" I will not move from here," she said firmly, " until you set all these poor people free."

It was night. Stealthy steps came into the yard. In the darkness Ma saw two men take away one of the mothers. She looked at the woman going to her death, and at the others, who pled with her to remain, for they feared this was a trick to get her away. What should she do ? Praying and hoping that she was right, she ran after the mother, and was just in time, for the woman was raising the poisoned water to her lips.

" Don't," cried Ma, and giving her a push she said, " Run." In an instant both jumped into the bush and made for Ma's hut.

" Quick," Ma cried to Mr. Ovens, " hide this woman."

He drew her in and piled up boxes against the door, and Ma ran swiftly back to the yard, where, to her joy, she found the other prisoners still safe. The warriors had been so astonished at what she had done that they had forgotten all about them.

Through more weary and exciting days the struggle went on. The chiefs at last said gloomily, " We will set some of the prisoners free and see if Ma will be satisfied." After giving a number a terrible native oath, and making them swear they were not guilty, they handed them over to Ma.

" Now," said the freemen, " we will kill the others."

" No," said Ma, and dared them to do such a dreadful thing.

They stormed and raged at her.

" We shall burn down the house and yard."

" All right," she retorted. " They are not mine."

More prisoners were released, and only three were left. Eme Ete came and knelt before her brother and begged him to set free one of them, a weak and timid creature, and this was done. A man and woman now remained, and Ma was resolved to save both. After a bitter struggle they let the man go, but nothing would make them give up the woman. She was doomed to death.

One afternoon Ma was secretly told that the funeral and the murder were to take place that night, and she was sick at heart. But when darkness fell, unknown hands —were they the hands of Eme Ete ?—cut the chains that bound the victim to the post, and with her leg irons on she crawled over the roof and found a refuge in Ma's room, from which, later, she fled to the freedom of the bush.

So the funeral of the young chief took place, but only a cow was killed and put into the coffin. No human blood was shed. It was the first time in the history of the tribe that such a wonderful thing had happened, and it was due to Ma's heroism and faith.

Two of the parties who went to the funeral met in the forest and quarrelled, and a man's head was cut off. War was declared, and there was much fighting before Ma got them to stop and settle the matter by palaver. " Blood for blood," was the verdict ; " the murderer must die." It was a custom of the natives that another could suffer in the place of one who was condemned. This man's friends offered his youngest brother, a little child, but the judge would not have him. Then a bigger brother was sent, and accepted. Before he could be killed, however, he escaped. One day Ma heard the sound of singing and joy-guns, and was told that he had been found and put to a cruel death before the eyes of his mother and sister.

A day or two afterwards loud screams filled the air. Ma rushed out and saw the women and children fleeing towards her yard.

"Egbo! Egbo!" they cried.

She listened, and heard the throb-throbbing of a drum. Egbo was a more dreadful thing in Okoyong than in Calabar, for there was no law against it. The men were dressed in leopards' skins and wore hideous masks, and carried long whips with which they flogged all whom they caught, and often killed them. Soon the village was filled with the queer figures, and shots were being fired. The women in the yard trembled in terror, and Ma prayed. By and by the noise died away, and on looking out she found that all had gone. Only one village had been destroyed. In revenge Edem armed his men, and they went after them, and shot down every straggler they came across.

Then arose another trouble. The brother of Edem, called Ekpenyong, was accused of slaying the dead lad Etim, and after drinking heavily he said he would take the poison ordeal to prove his innocence. When Ma arrived at his yard the women were clinging to him and trying to seize a bag which he held, and he was striking them fiercely.

"He has the beans in the bag, Ma," they cried.

She walked through the line of armed men who stood by.

"Give me the bag," she said quietly to the chief.

"No, Ma, there are only palm nuts and cartridges in it," he mumbled.

"Give it to me."

He threw it at her feet. She looked in and saw palm nuts and cartridges. Had he spoken the truth? But deep at the bottom she came upon two-score of the poison beans.

"I'll keep these," she told him.

"You will not! They are mine."

"Give them back," shouted the warriors.

Ma's heart beat wildly, but she walked down the ranks of the men, saying, "Here they are, take them."

They were so amazed at her courage that they let her pass, and she went and hid the beans in her house.

During the night Ekpenyong stole off to find more beans. Eme Ete sent Ma a secret message, and she rose and followed him, and coaxed him to take the native oath instead of the ordeal.

After all these wild doings the people came back to a better mind, and began to realise how brave and good Ma was; and at night, when she was alone with her bairns, they slipped in, one by one, and called her their great white mother, and thanked her with tears for all her love and devotion.

Edem, too, was softened, and the thought of vengeance left his heart. Ma prevailed upon him to allow the chief who had run away to return. Poor Akpo! His village had been burnt to the ground, and all his goats and fowls and goods were lost. But Edem gave him a new piece of land, and seed for food plants.

"Ah, Chief," said Ma, "that is the right way; that is the Jesus way."

"Thank you, Ma." And he, too, came and knelt before her, and held her feet and poured out his gratitude for all she had done.

"Go on, Ma," he said, "and teach us to do away with the bad old bush fashions. We are weary of them, they bind us like chains, and we need you to help us."

These words thrilled Ma with happiness, and were a reward for all she had come through; but they made her humble too, for she knew that unless God had been with her she would not have borne up so long.

Now that she was surer of herself and of that wondrous Power behind her, she grew bolder still, and went wherever trouble threatened. No place was too far for her to reach. Natives in distant parts were often surprised to see her walking into their midst when they were starting to fight. Once a secret message came, saying that two tribes, many miles away, were on the warpath. Ma was ill and weak and in bed, but she rose at once. Edem said, "Ma, you are going into a wild beast's den, and will not come out alive."

Night fell as she was tramping along, and she was always nervous of the darkness and the mystery of the forest. The animals frightened her. "I prayed," she said, "that God would shut their mouths, and He did." At midnight she reached a village where she hoped to borrow a drum and a freeman to beat it before her as she marched, a sign that one under the protection of Egbo was coming. But the chief, a surly despot, would not see her, and would not give her the drum.

"If there is a war," his message said, "a woman is not likely to stop it."

Back went her reply. "You think only of the woman. You have forgotten the woman's God. I go without a drum."

On she went, and came at last to one of the villages where the trouble was brewing. All was silent and still. Suddenly, out of the darkness swarmed armed men and closed around her and demanded her business.

"I have come to stop the war."

They jeered at her, such a small, feeble woman, and smiled grimly.

"You won't do that," they said.

"We shall see. I want to have a palaver and hear the story."

"All right, Ma," they replied, humouring her. "Go to sleep until second cock-crow, and we shall wake you up and take you with us." But when she was awakened the band were already away on their errand of death.

"Run, Ma, run and stop them!" cried the women, who feared what would happen; and she rushed breathlessly up and down steep tracks and through streams until she caught up with the warriors, who were making ready to attack and uttering their wild war whoops.

She walked into their midst.

"Don't go on like beardless boys," she said in scorn. "Be quiet."

Then she went on until she came upon the enemy drawn up in line across the path.

"I salute you," said she.

There was no reply. Why was this white woman interfering with them at such a moment?

"Oho! I see you are gentlemen and have nice manners."

They frowned. Things were looking dangerous, but Ma was never at a loss, and she began to smile and joke. Then stepped forward an old man and came and knelt at her feet.

"Ma, you know me? You remember you nursed and healed me?"

It was the sick chief she had gone to see after she arrived at Ekenge.

" Ma," he went on, " we confess that this quarrel is the fault of one of our foolish men, and it is a shame to bring evil on the whole town for one. We beg you to make peace."

Ma's heart thrilled with joy, and soon she had a number of men from each side talking over the matter. Often it seemed as if war must come after all, and it needed all her patience to make them agree, but at last it was decided that a fine should be imposed. To her horror this was paid at once in gin, and every one began to drink. She knew they would soon get violent and fight after all, and was almost in despair.

But taking off nearly all her clothes, she spread them over the boxes and bottles and dared any one to touch them. Only one glass would she give to each of the head men. So disappointed were the others that they surged round her in anger, but some of the older and wiser men obtained whips and made themselves into a bodyguard to protect her.

" If all of you go to your homes and don't fight," she said, " I'll promise to send the stuff after you."

They believed her, and trooped away like children.

It was night again when, worn out in body and mind, she tramped back through the dark and lonely forest, with crickets whistling and frogs croaking around her, and the little lamps of the fireflies pulsing in and out like the flashes of a lighthouse But there was a light in her own face that even the fireflies could not outshine.

Two years passed, two years of toil and hardship and strain. In the heat and rain, by day and night, Ma was never idle. If she was not tramping through the forest and putting down the customs of the people, she was busy with work about her own door, helping the women to sew and cook, teaching the children in school, preaching on weekdays and Sundays, and doctoring all who were ill. It was a marvel she kept at it so long. Perhaps it was because she had such a happy spirit, saw the funny side of things, and laughed at her troubles. She was always ready with a joke, even when lying ill in bed, and missionaries who went to see her usually found her as lively as a girl.

At this time she lived in a way that would have killed any other white person. She did not wear a hat or boots or stockings ; she went about thinly clad ; she ate the coarse food of the natives ; and although she was careful about the water she drank she did not filter or boil it, as all white people have to do in the Tropics. It made life simpler and easier, she said, not to bother about such things. How she did it no one knew ; the secret lay between her and God.

Even she, however, gave in at last. She became so ill that she was taken to Duke Town a wreck and carried on board the steamer and sent home. Janie again went with her, a woolly-headed lassie with velvet skin, and eyes that were always ready to laugh. She was beginning now to think that it would be a fine thing to be a white girl. One night, in a house in Glasgow when she was being bathed, she took the sponge and began to scrub the soles of her feet, which were whiter than the rest of her body. " Why are you doing that, Janie ? " she was asked. " Oh, because the white place is getting bigger, and if I scrub perhaps I'll be all white some day ! "

At this time Ma was dreaming another of her dreams. She wanted to see a place in Calabar where black boys could learn to use their hands as well as their heads, and so be able to become good workmen and teachers, and help to build up their country and make it rich and prosperous. She wrote a long letter to the Church magazine telling about her idea, and it was thought to be so good that the Church did what she asked it to do, and started a school which has grown into the great Hope-Waddell Training Institution, where boys are being taught all sorts of things.

Made strong by the home air and the love of new and kind friends, Ma fared forth again to her lonely outpost in the African backwoods.

The people of Ekenge were glad to see their white mother back, and confessed that they did not seem able to do without her. They came to her like children with all their troubles and sorrows, and she listened to their stories and advised and comforted them. When they quarrelled they said, " Let us go to Ma," and she heard both sides and told them who was wrong and who was right, and they always went away content.

She needed no longer to go to any of the villages round

about when a chief died. She just sent a message that there must be no killing. There was a great uproar, but back always came the reply, "We have heard. Our mother has made up her mind. We will obey." They did not know that Ma all the time was in her room kneeling and praying to God.

Some mourned over the old ways. "Ah, Ma," they sighed, "you have spoilt all our good fashions. We used to take our people with us when we went to the spirit land; now we must go alone."

But she had still to be on the alert, for many of the tribes at a distance from Ekenge had not yet given up their dark practices, and whenever they were bent on anything wicked they plunged deep into the heart of the forest to escape her eyes.

One day she heard that a chief had died, and was guided to one of these hidden spots, where she found his free men giving the poison ordeal to a number of prisoners. They thought she would grow tired and go away if they simply sat and waited, but days and nights passed and she remained with them, sleeping on the ground beside a fire. Of the armed men lying around her she was not afraid, but only of the wild beasts that might come creeping up through the darkness and leap upon her. It was not she who became wearied and hungry, but the men themselves, and by and by the prisoners were set free.

Eme Ete helped her most. It was she who told her when wrong-doing was being plotted. In the swift way that only natives know about, Eme Ete received news of it. Calling a trusty messenger she gave him a special kind of bottle.

"Take that to Ma and ask her to fill it with ibok (medicine)—go quick!"

When the messenger arrived at the Mission House and Ma saw the bottle, she knew what it meant. It said to her, "Be ready!" and she would not undress until she heard the cry, "Run, Ma, run!" Once she lay down to rest in her clothes for a whole month before word came, and then she saved the life of a man.

Sometimes a quarrel arose so quickly, and the call was so sudden, that she was not ready to go, and so she took a large sheet of paper and wrote anything on it that came to her mind, and after splashing some sealing-wax on it to make it look important, she sent it off by a swift runner. None of the fighting men could read, and by the time they had fingered it and talked over it Ma appeared.

She liked best, however, to appeal to the good side of the chiefs, and get them to meet and reason and settle their affairs themselves. She called it the Jesus way ; they called it the God-woman way ; learned men would call it " the art of self-government."

One of these palavers was in a green glade in the forest four miles away. The chiefs of the two tribes, who sat opposite each other under coloured umbrellas, were dressed in gorgeous clothes and ringed round by armed men. Ma took her place between them and began to knit, for the natives love to talk, and she knew the palaver would be a long one. Besides, she never felt quite so nervous when she knitted. First one spoke and then another, and the long hours passed, and Ma's back began to ache, but still the talking went on, and the excitement rose to fever-heat. Darkness fell with a rush, and torches were lit and threw a weird light on the scene.

" Enough ! " cried Ma. " Come, let us end."

An old chief went over all that had been said, and Ma gave the verdict, which pleased both sides.

Then, as was the custom, a warrior from each party stood forward, blood was drawn from their hands and mixed with salt and pepper and corn ; and half being given to one man and half to the other, they swallowed their portions at the same moment. This was the terrible blood covenant sealing the peace between tribes, and none ever dared to break it.

The sitting had lasted ten hours, and Ma was tired and hungry, but she walked back in the moonlight feeling very happy.

So with a love that never wearied, with a patience that never gave in, with a humour that never failed, Ma gradually put down the evil order of things far and near. Year by year she grew in power, and from her house ruled over thousands of people. She was really the Queen of Okoyong. This was a marvellous thing, for at that time all the country belonged to chiefs, and they could do as they liked.

By and by a change came, and Britain took charge of

the land and placed Consuls in the various districts. When Ma heard of it, she said: "You mustn't send one here. If you do there will be trouble, for my people are proud and fierce, and will fight."

"Well, Miss Slessor," the Government replied, "you know them best. Why not do the work yourself?"

And she did. She became what Dr. Livingstone had been. He always wore a blue cap with a gold band to show that he was a British Consul. Ma did not wear a hat, but she acted as a Consul, started a native court, and, like Deborah of old, judged the people and guided them about the new laws that were put into force. It was the first time in the history of our Empire that a woman had done such things. The result was all for good. Wild and lawless as the people were, they obeyed Ma, and so the rule of Britain over them began in peace.

Ma always bore herself with queenly dignity, but she was really very humble. She only did the work because she thought it was what Jesus wanted her to do. "I am only a poor weak woman," she said, "and not a Queen at all." The officials of the Government knew better; when they went to visit her they were amazed at the power she held over the people, and the deep respect and admiration they felt for her.

"She is a miracle," they exclaimed, "this white Queen of Okoyong."

CHAPTER V

Ma's great love for children; her rescue of outcast twins from death; the story of little Susie, the pet of the household; and something about a new kind of birthday that came oftener than once a year.

MA'S house at Ekenge was always like a big nursery.

Mothers are much the same all over the world, but in Africa they are very ignorant and thoughtless, and do not know how to care for their children, while they believe so much in the strange customs of the country that things are done to the little ones which seem to us hard-hearted and cruel. It was worse in Ma's days, when most of the people were still slaves.

She was always sorriest for the babies, they were so

helpless, and the only times she was really angry were when she saw them neglected or starved or made drunk. Then she was like a tigress, and the people fled before her. "Poor wee helpless things," she would say as she picked them up and thought of the way the white babies at home were cared for. She saw in the tiniest babe one for whom Jesus died; and she loved them all, and washed them and nursed them, and sang to them day and night.

There was no cradle in the Mission House, but something better. Ma's bed was in the middle of the room, and around it were hammocks slung to the roof, from each of which a cord was hung In these were placed the babies, and if any one became wakeful during the night and cried she would pull the string and set its hammock swinging, and soon the little one was slumbering again. Sometimes she had to look after half a dozen or more at once, and two or three hammocks would be going at the same time.

With many she had a hard struggle, but never grudged any trouble to make them well. She would come home late after a long day's tramp in the forest, tired and hungry and sleepy, and send Janie to bed and stay up herself and tend the sick and suffering ones. You can fancy her there alone in the mud-house in the forest in the quiet hours of the night, bending over a wasted form, watching the pain in its eyes with tears in her own, giving it medicine, soothing it, and seeking to make it comfy, and beside her the pale dark shape of Death, with its grim smile, waiting for another victim.

Ma sometimes won the child from the grave; sometimes she failed, and then she was very sad. But she could not help it. The people believed that sickness was caused by evil spirits, and most of the children that came to her were already dying and beyond her love and skill. When they closed their eyes she dressed them in a pinafore and put them in a box covered with white flowers, and buried them in her children's cemetery.

Some women who called at Ma's yard were gossiping about the day's marketing, when one said it was funny that a baby should live after being five days and six nights in the bush.

"What's that?" demanded Ma. "What do you mean?"

"Nothing, Ma. The girl baby that was thrown away because the mother is dead is still alive, for we heard her crying as we came along this morning."

Ma jumped up and went flying to the spot. She found the waif on some waste ground, terribly thin and eaten by insects and crying feebly. Taking her home Ma laid her in a big calabash and brooded over her with tender care, and by and by she recovered, and became healthy and pretty. "The child of wonder," the people called her; but Ma named her Mary, after herself, and she became one of her house-children, and stayed with her until she married.

Twins gave Ma the sorest time. The people believed that all sorts of troubles would come to them if these were allowed to live. Ma laughed at them.

"Twins are just like other children," she said; "and if only you let them grow up you will see for yourselves that there is no difference. Look at my bonnie Janie—she is a twin."

But it was no use. So the only thing for her to do was to save the little mites before they could be murdered. It was Eme Ete who told her when twins came, and when she got the secret message she dropped the work she was doing and made swiftly for the spot. Sometimes they were already dead and thrown away in pots, and the mother driven into the backwoods. If she were in time she took the infants home and nursed them and guarded them from the father and relatives, who usually tried to steal and destroy them.

One day she saved twins in her own village, and took them into the Mission House and put them in her bed. The people were alarmed, and said that dreadful things would happen. Chief Edem kept away. "I cannot go any more to my Mother's house," he groaned; "no, never any more." No one spoke to her. Mothers kept their children out of her way. She was sad and sorrowful, but she would not give in, for she knew she was doing right.

One of the twins died, but the other grew and waxed strong. The people liked their Ma so much that they, too, were unhappy at the cloud that had fallen between, and at last they began to make friends.

"Ma, forgive us," they said humbly. "We have not been taught right. Let your heart warm to us again."

So the shadow passed away. What cheered Ma most of all was that the father of the twin carried it home, and took back the mother, which showed that the old stupid notion was beginning to die.

Another day there was a great uproar. Twins had come to a slave woman, called Iye, about five miles off. Ma met her in the forest carrying the infants in a box on her head, a howling mob of men and women hounding her on. They had destroyed all her property and torn up her clothes. Ma took the box, because no one would touch it, and helped the poor mother along to the Mission House. They could not go by the usual path, as the villagers would not have used it afterwards, so they had to wait in the hot sun until another lane was cut.

The boy twin was dead, but the girl was alive, and with care became plump and strong. She was a bonnie child with a fair skin and sweet ways, and she became the pet of the household. Ma called her Susie, after her elder sister, and loved her as much as if she had been her own. Even the mother, after she got well and went away, sometimes came back to see her, and was proud of her good looks.

Fourteen months passed. One day Janie went upstairs to put a child to sleep, and asked Mana, one of the girls, to look after Susie, as she was full of play and mischief. Mana took her, and while getting the tea ready, placed a jug of boiling water on the floor for a moment. Susie, babylike, seized it and spilt the water over her bare body. She was dreadfully scalded. Ma was frantic, and for a fortnight scarcely let her out of her arms. Often the child smiled up in her face and held up her wee hand to be kissed. Ma at last carried her down to Creek Town, and woke up the doctor there at midnight in the hope that something more could be done. But the shock and wounds had been too severe, and when Ma got back the bright life of the queen of the household flickered and went out.

Ma's grief was pitiful, and made even the people wonder. " See how she loved her," they said one to another. They came and mourned with her, and stood by at the burial. Susie was robed in white, with her own string of beads round her neck, and a white flower in her hand.

It was very lonesome for Ma afterwards. " My heart aches for my darling," she wrote. " Oh, the empty place and the silence and the vain longing for the sweet voice and the soft caress and the funny ways. Oh, Susie! Susie!"

Her heart went out towards Iye, the slave mother, and by and by she bought her for £10 and made her free, and she remained in the Mission House, a faithful worker, and a great help to Ma and those who came after her.

All the stories of Ma's adventures with twins cannot be told, because she had to do with hundreds of them, but this is one which shows what she had often to go through.

One afternoon when she was busy teaching in the school a message was thrown suddenly at her from the door.

"Ma! come, twins."

"Where?" she asked.

"Twelve miles away in the bush, and the mother is very ill."

Ma went to the door and looked up. "There is going to be a storm," she said, "and I have a sickly baby to look after and night will soon be here, but—come along, Janie, we'll go."

Darkness fell ere they reached the spot, and the stars were hidden behind clouds, and they could hardly see a yard in front.

They found the woman lying unconscious on the ground. One of the infants was dead, and Janie dug a hole and buried it. Ma ordered the husband and his slave to make a stretcher, which they did very unwillingly. Then she placed the woman on it and bade them carry her. Still more unwillingly, and grumbling all the time—for they dreaded to touch a twin-mother—they obeyed. Janie lifted the living twin, and all set forth by the light of a piece of fire-stick glowing at the end. This went out, and they stumbled along in the dense darkness. At last they stopped. They had lost themselves. The men laid down their burden and went off to grope for a trail, and Ma and Janie were alone in the eerie forest with the moaning form at their feet.

"Oh, Ma, they may not come back," cried Janie.

"Well, my lassie, we'll just bide where we are until morning."

A shining ghostly thing leapt about in the darkness. Janie's heart went to her mouth. But it was only the men back with a torch made of palm tassel and oil which they had got from a hut. They went on again.

When the Mission yard was reached the men were so tired that they fell down and went to sleep at once. Ma, too, was tired, but her work was not done. She got a hammer and nails and some sheets of iron and knocked up a little lean-to, in which she put the woman and nursed her back to consciousness, and fed and comforted her. Then, utterly worn out, she just lay down where she was in her soiled and damp clothes, and fell sound asleep.

The baby died next day, and the mother grew worse, and there was no hope. She was sore in spirit as well as in body, and sorrowed for her fate and the loss of her husband's love. Ma soothed her, and told her she was going to a better world, where no one would be angry with her for being a twin-mother.

When she passed away the people would not touch or come near her, and so Ma did all that was needful herself, and placed her in a coffin, and then the husband and his slave bore her away and buried her in a lonely spot in the bush.

Poor twin-mothers of Africa!

Though Ma did not save very many of the twin-children that passed through her hands, she did a great work by making the people realise how foolish and sinful a thing it was to be afraid of them and kill them.

The household had grown and grown. We know about Janie and Mary, both trickified and bright little maidens. Then there was Mana, a faithful and affectionate lassie. One day, in her own country, she had gone to the spring for water, and was seized by two men and brought to Okoyong and sold to Eme Ete, who gave her to Ma. Wee Annie was there also, very shy and timid, but a good nurse. Her parents had stolen and eaten a dog in the bush, and there was much trouble, and the mother died, and Annie would have been buried in the grave had not Ma taken her. Six other boys and girls with sad stories also lived in the Mission House, so that Ma often felt she was like the old woman who lived in a shoe, and who had so many children she didn't know what to do.

It was not easy for her to keep in stock the food and medicine and clothes that were needed for the family, and sometimes she would run out of things. Once, when she was short of tins of milk, she strapped a baby on her back and tramped down the forest trail to Creek Town, got what she wanted, and patiently tramped back again.

Another time she was watching some women who were imprisoned within a stockade and were going to be killed, and as she could not leave the place Janie handed her cups of tea through the fence. Suddenly a tornado came on and flooded the Mission House and soaked all the clothes. Ma herself was wet to the skin. To add to her trouble Janie came and said, "Ma, we have no milk, and the baby is crying for some."

"Well, Janie, I'll just have to trot to Creek Town for it. I'll get some dry clothes too. Put the baby in a basket."

Slipping out in the darkness, and taking a woman to help to carry the baby, she set forth. They lost their way in the rain, and wandered hither and thither, and only reached the town at the dawning of the day. Ma roused one of the ladies of the Mission, obtained the milk and a change of clothes, and lay down for a little sleep. Hearing that she had come, King Eyo got his canoe ready, and sent her back by the river. Her absence from the stockade had not been noticed, and she was able later to settle the trouble without bloodshed.

There were plenty of merry days in the home-life of Ekenge. Wherever girls are gathered together there is sure to be fun and laughter, and Ma had always the heart and will of a girl for jokes and mischief. She could not take her bairns into lighted streets or gay shops, or to places of amusement, for there was none of these things in the bush, but sometimes she gave them a holiday, and a special tea, and gifts. Perhaps, however, the most delightful treat they had was when a box arrived from across the sea.

All over Scotland loving hearts were thinking of Ma, and loving hands were working for her; and clothing, books, pictures, and knick-knacks were being collected and packed in boxes and sent out addressed to her in Okoyong. The Sunday School children also had their thoughts on the Mission, and gave their pennies and halfpennies to it just as Ma herself had done when a little girl. About this time they gathered up enough money to build a steel steamer for use on the inland rivers and creeks, and it was now plying up and down, carrying mails and parcels and missionaries. It was called the *David Williamson*, after a minister of the Church who visited Calabar, but the natives named it the *Smoking Canoe*.

You can imagine the excitement at the Mission House at Ekenge when a half-naked messenger, his dark body perspiring and glistening in the sun, appeared, and cried:

" Ma, the *Smoking Canoe* is at the beach."

" Ho-ho! gifts from Makara land," sang half a dozen throats. " Oh, Ma, when can we go? Let us go now."

Ma was as excited as the rest, so off went men, women, and children, streaming along the path to the river, where the *David Williamson* lay.

As the boxes were usually too heavy to be carried, they were opened up on the beach and the contents made into parcels. These the natives balanced on their heads and went off, a long file of them, through the forest to Ekenge. Sometimes it needed a second and a third journey before all the goods were together again.

What a delight it was to Ma to open the packages! What cries of rapture came from the children and the people looking on as they saw all the things that were to them so wonderful and beautiful.

There were print garments by the dozens, woollen articles, caps, scarves, handkerchiefs, towels, ribbons and braids, thimbles, needles and pins, beads, buttons, reels, spoons, knives, scrap-books, picture-books and cards, texts, pens, and a host of other things. It was almost with awe that the women touched the pretty baby-clothes, and the men clapped their hands as Ma held up a blue or scarlet gown or jacket.

The dolls were looked upon as gods, and Ma would not give them away in case they were worshipped: she kept the prettily dressed ones to teach the women and girls how clothes were made and how they were worn. Some common things, which children at home would not value, they treasured. When Janie was handed a penwiper, " Oh, Ma," she said reproachfully, " wipe a dirty pen with that? No, no." And she put it up on the wall as an ornament!

One old woman was given a copy of the picture " The Light of the World." " Oh," she cried in joy, " I shall never be lonely any more!"

If you had watched Ma closely when she was opening the

packages, you would have seen that she was seeking for something with a quick and impatient eye. When at last she found what she wanted she gave a shout of triumph. Tins of home-made toffee and chocolate! They were always there, for every one knew she liked sweets. When at home she used to ask that these might be sent out, because the bush bairns were fond of them, but her friends just laughed in her face. "Miss Slessor," they would say, "you can eat as many as the bairns!" "Of course I can," she confessed.

After the children had looked at all the gifts Ma would tell them where they came from, and would kneel down and thank Jesus for putting it into the hearts of the givers in Scotland to care for His forlorn black folk in Africa.

Then Ma said, "Away to bed, bairns. But oh, hasn't it been grand? It's just been like a birthday. Many happy returns!"

Ma did not give all the things away. A brilliant gown might go to the chief as a gift—and he would sit proudly in Court with it and be admired and envied by all—or a flannelette garment to some poor and aged woman to keep her warm during the shivery fog season; but as a rule Ma liked the people to work for what they got, or to pay something for them. Thus she taught them to want clothes and other things, and showed them how to get them, and in this way she was a real Empire builder. She used to say that there was no truer or more successful Empire maker than the missionary.

CHAPTER VI

How the Queen of Okoyong brought a high British official to talk to the people; how she left her nice home and went to live in a little shed; how she buried a chief at midnight; how she took four black girls to Scotland, and afterwards spent three very lonely years in the forest.

THE tribes in some of the out-of-the-way places were apt to forget that British law was now the law of the land, and go back to the old habits that were so deep-rooted in their nature. Ma often threatened that she would have to make them feel the power that stood behind her. Once, when the land of a widow was stolen, she asked the people whether they would have the case judged by God's law or by the Consul and a gun? After a while they said, "Iko Abasi—God's word."

Ma opened her Bible and read: "Thou shalt not remove thy neighbour's landmark—that is God's law"; and the land was returned to the woman.

Then a chief died, and the blame was laid on one who was innocent. As a tornado was blowing, Ma could not visit the district, but she sent a message:

"I'll come and see about it when the rain goes off."

"Oh, yes," the people grumbled, "and when she comes she won't allow us to give the prisoners the bean. Let us take away the man and hide him."

And they hurried him to a spot deep in the forest beyond her reach.

Ma was vexed, and she was ill and tired. "I am not going to hunt for them this time," she said quietly. "They must learn to obey the law, and I will give them a lesson."

So she wrote to the Government at Duke Town, asking them to send up some one to deal with the matter, and she took the letter herself to the beach, and dispatched it by a special canoe.

Nothing can be hidden in negroland, and the news of what she had done soon reached the disobedient people. They came out of the forest in as great a hurry as they went in, and rushed to the Mission House.

"Where is Ma? We want Ma."

"Ma," said Janie crossly, "is away for the Consul. I hope he will bring a big gun with him. It's time. You are killing her with your silly ways."

They went back sorrowful and alarmed, for a big gun meant ruined homes and crops, and many arrests, and imprisonment down at the coast. When they saw Ma later, they begged her to ask the Consul to come with thoughts of peace and not of war.

"Good," she replied, "and we shall have a proper big palaver about all your bad customs."

When the Government official with his guard of soldiers arrived, he was amused to find the Queen of Okoyong sitting bareheaded on the roof of her house repairing a leak. She came down, and they had a palaver with the chiefs and people, who promised not to do any more killing at funerals, and not to murder twins.

Ma shrugged her shoulders. "They will promise anything," she told the officials. "I'll have to keep a close eye on them all the same."

She did ; and as they broke their word she brought up the Consul-General himself, Sir Claude Macdonald. He spoke kindly, but firmly, to the chiefs.

"The laws are made for your good and safety and peace, and if you do not obey them you will be punished."

They agreed to all he said. "Sir, when words are spoken once, we don't mind them ; but when they are spoken twice, we obey."

Ma also addressed them, telling of the blessings that would follow obedience, and of the quiet and happy days they would enjoy long after she had gone.

"Ma ! Ma !" they cried in alarm, "you must not leave us ! You are our Mother, and we are your children. God must not take you from us until we are able to walk by ourselves."

After that things were better, though Ma's life did not grow less hard. Indeed it was more stirring than ever. For various reasons her people were leaving their huts and building new ones at a place called Akpap, and Ma had to shut up the Mission and go with them.

The only house she could find to live in was a little shed like a two-stalled stable, or one of the sheep-houses you see on the Scottish hills, with a mud floor and no windows. But she did not mind. She always thought of her Master, who had not a place to lay His head. So she put her boxes in one end, and in the other she lived and slept with the children.

It was a grand play-ground for rats, lizards, ants, beetles, and other jumping and creeping things. At night the rats ran over Ma, and played hide-and-seek in the roof. Once, when Mr. Ovens arrived to do some carpentry work, he went to wash himself in the shed. In the dimness he felt what he thought was a sponge floating in the basin, and saying Ma was surely getting dainty, he used it for his face, only to find that it was a drowned rat !

From this lowly hut, as from a palace, Ma continued to rule Okoyong.

Soon a strange disease seized her new lot of babies, and four died from it. Then smallpox, that dreadful scourge, swept through the land, and so many of her people were carried off that they lay unburied in their huts. Ma was busy from dawn till dark, and often from dark again till dawn, vaccinating the well ones, and nursing the ill and the dying.

To her great grief her old friend, Chief Edem, caught the disease. In spite of his faults, which, after all, were the faults of his African upbringing, he had been very good to her, and she was grateful for all he had done. When she reached his hut at Ekenge there was no one with him, for as soon as a man or a woman was stricken all others fled. She fought the disease through long weary hours, but was not able to save him, and he died in the middle of the night. Tired as she was, and weak from lack of sleep, and alone, she felt that she could not let him lie like that. Going out she got some wood and made a coffin. Then in the darkness she dug a grave and buried him. There was no dancing and drinking and killing as this chief of Okoyong entered the spirit-land, only the faint noises of the forest, and the stillness of the starry sky, and a woman's mute prayer. When all was done she dragged her wearied body back in the cool of the dewy dawn to Akpap.

Was it a wonder that she began to lose her strength? Fevers laid her low, and illnesses, due to lack of good food, weakened her. She could scarcely crawl about. Yet she would not give in, and bravely drudged away at her work. At last the other missionaries said, " Ma, if you don't go home, you will die." She did not want to die : she wanted to live, and do much more for Jesus. " If," she said, " a holiday will help me, I will go. But what shall I do with my girls? I cannot leave Janie, Mary, Alice, and Maggie here. If I go I must take them with me."

Her friends were astonished.

" How can you take four black girls to Scotland, and you so ill, Ma? It is impossible."

" God can do impossible things," she replied in simple faith. " He will keep me and take care of them."

" What about your clothes? " they asked.

" We have none but the old things we have on : the ants have eaten up the rest. But God will provide what we need."

Sure enough, when they went to Duke Town a box arrived from a Glasgow church, and in it was all the nice warm clothing they required.

It was the same everywhere. Kindness fell on her like sunshine. At Liverpool she handed her purse to a railway porter, and he bought the tickets and fixed them up in a carriage. And at Edinburgh there was a faithful friend, Mrs. M'Crindle, on the platform, waiting to take the whole family to her home in Joppa.

"Isn't God good to me?" she often said, with a happy smile.

The four African foundlings were stared at by the rosy-cheeked boys and girls, who, however, were kind to them when they heard their sad stories. None except Janie knew a word of English, but they were all clever, and soon picked it up, and Mary even went to school in Portobello.

After a happy time Ma took a house of her own at Seton Mill, where she got a glimpse of the sea, and here they all lived as in Africa, Janie being cook, and Ma going about often bare of foot and bare of head. But life in Scotland is not like what it is in the wilds of the Tropics, and Ma was sometimes found shivering over the fire. So a fairy god-mother, in the shape of Miss Adam, a lady of the Church who loved her, carried them off to a lovely village in the south called Bowden, where they stayed all July and August.

A little girl named Happy Gray, who was staying with Miss Adam, grew very friendly with the children, and together they wandered through the fields and woods, gathering flowers and raspberries, or climbed the Eildon Hills. They taught Happy how to burst "cape gooseberries" on the back of her hand, and showed her that when they gathered nettles they did not feel any sting. With her they drove to Stitchel Manse, where they ate apple tarts in the summer-house, and also went to St. Mary's Loch, the four black faces being a wonder to all the people in the countryside.

After a time Ma left this haunt of peace to go and speak at meetings, for she was a famous person now, and every one was eager to see and hear the wonderful pioneer who lived alone amongst savages. She was very shy, and would not open her mouth if men were listening, and if any one began to praise her she would run away. It was always the work she spoke about, and the need for more women and girls to go out and help.

Once in Edinburgh she was coaxed to address a meeting in the Synod Hall. " I dinna ken how I'm to do it," she said to a friend. " You'll pray for me ? Where will you sit ? " Her friend said, " In the gallery." " I'll look for you, and ken you are praying, and that will help."

And, as usual, she spoke well. By and by many students of the Church College came creeping in under the gallery and listened, and she did not seem to mind, but appealed to them too, saying, " There are many students who are ready, and making ready, to serve Jesus, and to tell about Him, and they will be running after fine churches and good manses, but there are multitudes who have never heard of Jesus out yonder. And for His sake will they not come out and work for Him there ? "

Sometimes she spoke of the good of prayer. " If you are ever inclined to pray for a missionary, do it at once, wherever you are," she said ; " perhaps she may be in great peril at the moment. Once I had to deal with a crowd of warlike men in the compound, and I got strength to face them because I felt that some one was praying for me just then."

At another meeting, when Mary with her bright happy face was with her, she told the young people how to be real ladies and gentlemen. " It is not," she said, " the wearing of fine clothes, or the possession of great wealth, but having gentle manners and kind consideration for the feelings and happiness of others—not the giving of our money or the denying of ourselves of small luxuries to help the coming of the Kingdom, but the cheerful daily giving of ourselves for the good of others at home and abroad."

She was most at home with children, and at her best at the tea-table, or when she curled herself up on the rug in front of the fire. Then came fearsome stories that made them tremble—true stories of what she had seen and done in dark Okoyong.

" Oh, mother," the children would say when being tucked in bed, " how can Miss Slessor live alone like that with wild men and wild beasts and everything ? "

" Ah," was the soft reply, " she does it because she loves

Jesus, and wants to help Him. I wonder, now, if you could love Him as much as that ?"

And the little minds in the little heads that were snuggling down amongst the comfy pillows also wondered.

Ma was a puzzle to the grown-ups, too, for they saw that she was not only very shy but very timid. Some small girls had more courage than she. She would not cross a field that had a cow in it : she was nervous in the streets, and usually got some one to take her across from side to side. She had not even the nerve to put up her hand to stop a car : she would take one only if it were standing. She shook when in a boat or sitting behind a fast horse.

Why was she afraid in this way ? Just because these things happened to herself. In big things, where the cause of Jesus was in danger, or others were to be protected and saved from hurt, she forgot her own feelings, and thought only what was to be done, and was braver and stronger even than men. Her heart was so loving that she was willing to die in the service of Jesus. You remember what He said, "Greater love hath no man than this, that a man lay down his life for his friends." That was her kind of love—the kind which Jesus Himself had for the world, which made Him do so much for us, and which led Him at last to His awful agony on the Cross.

She should have stayed a year, but when the winter came on with grey, cold, weeping skies, she and the bairns missed the sunshine and heat. Ah ! and she was always thinking of the work to be done in Africa. To her friends who pressed her to stay, she said, "If ye dinna send me back, I'll swim back. Do you no ken that away out there they're dying without Jesus ?" So they set sail and spent Christmas Day at sea.

What a reception they got at Akpap ! "Everything will be right now," the people said, "Ma is back." And once more she became the sovereign lady of Okoyong.

The next three years were the loneliest and worst she ever spent in the forest. She was never once down in Calabar, few white persons came to see her, and she had a big battle to fight with ill-health. There was not a day that she did not suffer weakness and pain : for whole nights she never slept, for months she was low with fever, and at times she believed she was going to die. Think what it must have been for her to lie there alone, tended only by her black girls. But she was never in the dumps. Somehow her spirit always managed to conquer her body, and she would struggle up and with a droll smile and a stout heart go on with her work. Nobody knew all she did in those years, for the story is hidden behind a veil of silence; only now and again we get a glimpse of her, lit up for a moment, as by a flash of lightning, and she is always bravely fighting for Jesus and the right, now hurrying to rescue twins and orphans, now sallying out to some village to put down the drinking, now travelling far to save life.

When she was not doing these things she was busy about her own doors. She had now a new house with a room underneath, and here she taught the day-school and held services and Bible classes and preached on Sundays. And there were always the Court and the palavers and the dispensary and the building and repairing and cooking and digging and a hundred and one other duties. So absorbed, indeed, did she get in what she was doing that often, as in the early days at home, she lost count of time. Sometimes she did not know what day of the week it was. Sundays had a habit of getting mixed up with other days. Once she was found holding her services on a Monday thinking it was Sunday, and again on a Sunday she was discovered on the roof hammering away in the belief that it was Monday.

She ruled with a firm but kindly hand. The hard and terrible times she had come through had changed her a little. She had still the old sweetness, but she could be stern, and even rough, with the people, and she often spoke to them in a way which a white man would not have dared to do. Those who were brought up to Court for harming women she punished severely. If any chief challenged what she said, she would take off the slipper she had put on as part of her simple Court dress, and slap him over the bare shoulder with it.

Yet she was never afraid. She went about alone by day and night, and never carried a weapon. She had no locks on her doors. Once a murderer was caught and nearly torn to pieces by the mob before he was chained and brought to Ma to be judged. She heard the evidence, and ordered him to be sent down to Duke Town for trial. Then she took off his irons, and sent away the guard, and bade him come into the house, where she sat down and talked to him earnestly for a long time. He was a big man, violent and sullen, and he could easily have knocked her down and escaped into the woods. But he listened quietly, and allowed her to lead him to the room below, where she fastened him in for the night.

Only once in all the years she spent in Okoyong was she struck, and that was by accident. There was a quarrel and a fight, and she went into the press of excited men to stop them. One of the sticks hit her. A cry of horror arose:

"Ma is hurt! Our Ma is hurt!"

Both sides at once fell on the wretched man who held the stick, and began to beat him to death.

"Stop, stop!" Ma cried. "He did not mean to do it."

And it was only by using all her strength and forcing them back that she saved his life.

And so the years wore on, and the new century came. "A new century," said Ma, sitting dreaming in her lonely little house. "What will it hold? It will at least hold His loving kindness and care all the way through, and that is enough."

For fifteen long patient years Ma gave her life to Okoyong, and she had her reward, for it became a land of peace and order and good will, the bad old customs died away, and the people were slowly but surely becoming the disciples of Jesus.

It was a wonderful thing for a white woman to have done alone, but Ma would not take any credit for it; she said it was no power of her own that had won her such a place in the heart of the wild people: it was the power of Jesus working in her and through her. *He* was the King of Okoyong, and she was only His humble servant-maid.

CHAPTER VII

Tells of a country of mystery and a clever tribe who were slave-hunters and cannibals, and how they were fought and defeated by Government soldiers; how Ma went amongst them, sailing through fairyland, and how she began to bring them to the feet of Jesus.

On some quiet summer day you may have been wandering through a country lane when you suddenly felt a whiff of perfume, fresh and sweet, and wondered where it could have come from. You looked about, but there was nothing save a tangle of green wood. You searched the hedges, and went down to the brown stream below the bridge and along its banks. The fragrance was still scenting the air, now strong, now faint, but you could not find its source. Then suddenly you came upon it—a sweetbriar bush, hidden away in a lonely and lowly spot.

Ma Slessor was like this modest briar bush. The influence of her goodness spread far and near, and the fame of her doings reached peoples who lived hundreds of miles away. They said to one another, " Let us go and see this wonderful White Mother "; and they left their villages and travelled through forests and across wide rivers and creeks, risking capture and death at the hands of hostile tribes, to seek her advice and help. Some of these visitors spoke languages Ma did not understand, and they had to talk to one another in signs. Chiefs in districts she had never heard of sent her messages: " Oh, Great White Mother, come and dwell with us, and we will be God-men." Escaped slaves from cannibal regions, who had been doomed to be eaten, fled to her for refuge. All received from her a kind welcome and food, and, best of all, had a talk about the Divine Chief who was to be the real Saviour of Africa.

There were other visitors to Okoyong she liked less, slave-dealers from beyond the Cross River, who brought women and girls to sell. A slow fire of rage had long been burning in Ma's heart against this cruel system, and sometimes it burst into fierce flame. She would hear a sound of bitter sobbing, and go out to see a string of naked little girls being driven forwards by a man carrying brass rods on his head—the money which the natives use. She would be so angry that she would shake her fist at the trader and storm at him, but he would only grin and ask her which girl she wanted, and would then describe their good points just as if they had been so many fowls or goats. Sometimes there would be sick ones, or ones suffering from ill-treatment, and these the dealers would leave, and she would nurse them back to health, though she was always very unwilling to let them go again into the awful whirlpool of slave-life.

She knew many of the dealers quite well, and often had long talks with them about the mysterious country from which they came. White men had not yet entered into the heart of it, but Ma learnt enough to be sure that it was a far more wicked place even then Okoyong had been. It was called Iboland, and one of the tribes, the Aros, were so cunning and clever that they had become a power over a vast region. It was they who were the slave-stealers, seeking their victims everywhere, and selling them in markets to the traders. One of their best hunting-grounds was Ibibio, the country to the south, where the natives were poor and naked and miserable, and lived in little settlements deep in the forest, because of their fear of the slave-raiders.

The Aros believed that they had a wonderful *chuku* or juju near a place now called Arochuku—which means the god of the Aros—in a rocky gorge down which a stream flowed. At one spot there was a pool overhung by trees and creepers. Here, amongst the white lilies, swam ugly cat-fish, with fierce-looking eyes, that were held to be sacred, and which it was death to catch. On a little island was a hut, guarded by priests, in which the juju was supposed to live. The people thought it could aid them in time of trouble, and came in great numbers to the shrine to ask advice and get their quarrels made up. Though the priests helped many in this way, they were cunning and greedy, and often acted very cruelly. They took the food and money which the visitors brought, and then said the juju wanted a living offering. So some poor man or woman was taken into the glen blindfolded, and the friends of the victim knew that the sacrifice was made by seeing the blood flowing past lower down.

Others who entered never came out again. The priests

said they had been seized by the juju, and the blood-red river seemed to show this, but a dye had been thrown in to colour the water. These persons were taken far away in secret, and sold into slavery. Any that were not of much value were slain and eaten in the cannibal feasts.

Now that Ma's dream of conquering Okoyong had come true, she was dreaming other dreams, and the most fascinating of these was to go to this terrible cannibal country and put down the evil doings of the natives. She told the slave-dealers about it.

"All right, Ma," they said, for they liked her, and admired her courage. "We, who know you, will be glad to welcome you; but we are not sure about the priests—they may kill you."

"I will risk that," she said; "as soon as I can get away from here you will see me."

In order to find out more about the tribes, she sometimes went far up the Cross River in a canoe, stopping wherever she could get shelter. On one of her journeys, when she had some of the house-children with her, the canoe was attacked by a huge hippopotamus. It rushed at the canoe, and tried to overthrow it. The men thrust their paddles down its throat and beat it, but it kept savagely nosing and gripping the frail vessel. Great was the excitement. Its jaws were snapping, the water was in a whirl of foam, the men were shouting and laying about them with their paddles, the girls were screaming, Ma was sometimes praying and sometimes giving orders. At last the canoe was swung clear, and paddled swiftly away.

The story of this adventure is still told in Calabar, and if you ask Dan, one of Ma's children, about it, he will say, "Once, when Ma was travelling in a canoe, she was attacked by hippopotamuses, but when they looked inside the canoe and saw her, they all ran away!"

What Ma saw and heard made her all a-quiver to go into these strange lands, but she would not leave the Okoyong people until some one came to take her place. The Mission had no other lady to send, and so she could only watch and pray and wait.

Matters became worse. The Aros hated the white rule, and would not submit to it. They tried to prevent the Government opening up their country to order and justice and peace, and would not allow the officials to enter it; they blocked the river so that no white vessel, or native one either, could pass; they went on with their slave-hunting and cannabalism. At last the Government lost patience. "We must teach them a lesson," they said. So a warning went to all the missionaries along the banks of the river to come down to Calabar at once. Ma Slessor did not like the order. "Everything is peaceful in Okoyong," she said. "My people won't fight." The Government said they knew that, but her life was too precious to risk, and they sent a special steamer for her and the children.

When she came she found several companies of soldiers, with many quick-firing guns, already moving up the river. They landed in the Aro country, and marched through swamps and attacked the hosts of natives who had gathered to bar their way, and defeated them. Still, the bushmen would not give in, and the soldiers had many a weary time in the trackless forests. At Arochuku they went down the gorge to the juju house, at the door of which they found a white goat starving to death. Many human skulls and cooking-pots lying about told a gruesome tale. The place continued to be the scene of wicked ceremonies, and was at last blown up with dynamite.

Ma was sorry she had not gone to Iboland before the soldiers, because she felt that if she had done so she might have saved all the fighting and bloodshed. Now that a way had been blazed into the country, she was more than ever eager and impatient to go.

"The Gospel should have been the first to enter," she said; "but since the sword and gun are before us, we must follow at once."

So while carrying on the work at Akpap, she began to explore and look out for some place that would do for an outpost. One day she left Akpap, taking with her the slave-girl Mana, who now knew English and her Bible well, and a bright boy called Esien, and tramped to the Cross River, where she boarded a canoe and paddled slowly up-stream. By and by she came to another smaller river on the west, which seemed to run far into the interior between Ibo and Ibibio, and there she landed on a beach at the foot of a hill. This was Itu, a famous place, for it was here that one of the greatest slave-markets in West Africa used to be held, and it was down this side river, the Enyong Creek, that the slaves were brought in canoes, to be sold and sent over the country, or shipped abroad to the West Indies or America.

"A good place to begin," Ma said; and she landed and climbed up the steep bank to the top, where she had a beautiful view over the shining river and the green land. "Oh, yes," she repeated, "a bonnie place to begin."

Once more she lived the gipsy life. She opened a school, made Mana and Esien the teachers, and started to build a church. The people, who had so long trembled in the shadow of slavery, were so pleased that they did all they could to help her, and the children of the village tumbled over one another in their eagerness to "learn book."

When she left for Akpap again the chiefs gave her the gift of a black goat, and she tied a piece of string to it and led it to the beach, where the Mission boat picked her up and took her down to the landing-place for Okoyong. She was bareheaded and barefooted, but in high spirits at the success of her trip, and she went away gaily into the forest, leading her goat and singing:

> Mary had a little lamb,
> Its fleece was white as snow!

Mana did a wonderful work at Itu: she taught the women and girls to read and sew, held prayers in the chief's yard every night, and preached on Sunday; and just because she loved Jesus, and tried to be like Ma, she soon had hundreds falling under the spell of the new way of life. This humble slave-girl did not fall away like others. She and Esien remained always true disciples of their Lord.

"If only some one would come and help me at Akpap," Ma prayed, and her wish was answered, for another brave woman, Miss Wright, one of the Mission agents in Calabar, offered to go up and stay with her, and after that everything was easy, for Ma Slessor loved Ma Wright, and Ma Wright loved Ma Slessor, and both loved the bairns, and the bairns loved both, so that it was a happy company which lived in this African forest clearing.

By this time Ma's own special family was complete, and no more members were added, so we can look in upon them and see who they were and what they did

First, of course, came Janie, who was now a big lassie, very kind, and full of sympathy for everybody. She spoke English fluently, and, like Ma, was a constant reader of the Bible; few white boys or girls, indeed, know it so thoroughly as she did. She was Ma's right hand, and could do almost anything, indoor or outdoor, clean, cook, carry a load, build a house, or work in the fields. But she liked working outside best, and, although a twin, had many friends amongst the people.

Mary was another good girl, though not so fond of hard work as Janie. She waited upon Ma, and did all her little ploys. Alice was a quiet, solid, plodding little soul, not as bright as Janie or Mary, but faithful in whatever duty she was given to do, and always willing and obedient. Annie had no head at all for her lessons, but was very diligent, and always smiling. Maggie the restless—Ma's name for her was Flibberty-gibbet—was the one who was fond of the babies, always busying herself about them, except when she was in the kitchen cooking a tit-bit for her own little mouth. The baby of the family was Whitie, a twin with dancing eyes, and giving promise of being clever by and by.

Then there were the two boys, Dan, a lively little fellow, not clever, but good, who had been brought up by Janie and was a favourite with Ma, and, as is often the case with a boy amongst a lot of sisters, was a little spoiled; and toddling Asoquö, who was so very fond of food that he sometimes stole the cat's milk!

In the house at this time was another boy named Impie. Poor Impie! He was deformed and could not use his legs, and the natives had some queer notion about it. He lay all day, so patient, with a smile for everybody; and when, in the evening, Ma Wright took him on her knee until bed-time, his face was a picture of perfect content. He died soon afterwards.

All the children were astir before six in the morning. Annie made up the wood fire and boiled water in the kettle for Ma's tea, and Janie or Mary prepared it and brought it in. Then they swept up the yard, and went into the bush to gather firewood or look for herbs to make *efere* or native soup. At prayers the children squatted on the verandah. They sang a hymn in English, and the bigger ones read verse about, Ma explaining as they went along—for she never hurried through worship no matter how busy she might be. Then she prayed in Efik, and all repeated the Lord's Prayer in English.

Prayers were not always at the same time, and sometimes when everybody was out of doors sweeping up or cutting down bush, Ma summoned them to the shade of a palm or cotton or orange tree, and had them there just to teach them that people could worship God anywhere—at their work, as well as in church.

" Boys and girls," she used to tell her young friends in Scotland, " should pray at their play or lessons as well as when reading or saying their prayers night and morning. Make a habit of it by looking up and saying a word or two in thought at any time. God is interested in our play and work and everything."

Then came lessons for a couple of hours, Ma doctoring patients or holding palavers the while. After breakfast the big lads or children from the village came, and school was held out in the open air under the verandah. This went on until six o'clock, when the evening meal was taken.

Prayers were again held on the verandah, and as the refugees in the yard and many of the neighbours came and sat below, the native tongue only was used. There was a hymn, and Ma would tell a simple gospel story, and all would say: " This night I lay me down to sleep." By that time one or two of the little ones were already in slumberland, and were carried off to bed.

On Sunday nights the hymns that children all over the world know were sung, sometimes with choruses which Ma made up herself; and instead of reading, the girls told what they remembered of the sermon. Janie was best at this. Mary and Alice could, at least, say the text, and when it came to Annie's turn she always said: " Nkokop nte Jesus edi eyen Abasi "—" I heard that Jesus is the Son of God."

Market-day was an exciting time for the children. The people came crowding in from the villages with all sorts of food and things to sell, such as yams—these are something like large potatoes—shrimps from the river, oil from the palm-nut, sugar-cane, ground nuts, Indian corn, and fowls.

Most of them came to see Ma, many simply to "köm" her, that is, to give her compliments, others to get advice or medicine. They brought little gifts for the children, sugar-cane, oranges and bananas and other fruit, or seed-plants, which they put in their own plots of ground, for they all liked to grow things.

It was Ma who taught them to love flowers. She knew a great deal about the wild plants of the forest. One day when walking with a visitor along the path, he complained of toothache, and by and by she picked a flower and told him to chew it. He did so, and the pain vanished. He plucked another which he thought was the same, and she said, "If you eat that you will be dead in five minutes."

Ma taught them many other things—indeed all they knew—and needed to be very patient, for think of the ages of darkness and ignorance that lay behind them! She tried, above all, to get them to hate lying, which is so common in Africa. Her one great and constant bit of advice and warning to them was—"Speak the truth."

These pleasant days in the Mission House were soon to end. Ma was now ready to go forward, and only waited to be sure that God was leading her, for she never wanted to go any way but His. One day she trudged the six miles to the Cross River in the hope of catching the Government launch for Itu. It passed when she was resting in a hut, and she had to trudge back the weary miles to Akpap again.

"Oh, Ma," said Miss Wright, "I am sorry you missed it."

Ma was tired, but only smiled and said, "Never mind, lassie, God did not mean me to go to-day, and He knows best."

A week later the launch saw her and picked her up, and on board she found the Military Commander.

"Ma," he said, "I'm going as far as Arochuku. Why not come up with me?"

"Oh," she thought, "is this what God meant when He turned me back last week?" And although she meant only to go to Itu and had no change of clothing or food, she said, "Yes, I will go."

And so she passed Itu and sailed up the Enyong Creek, one of the loveliest little waterways in the world. She had seen many beautiful bits of tropical scenery, but never one so beautiful as this. At first it is broad and open, and here and there she saw a tiny canoe with a man fishing for shrimps, and she was told that electric fish, which gave one a shock, lived in the water. Then it ran through the forest, where it was as still as a lake in the heart of the hills and dark and green because the branches drooped over it. Through the little arches of foliage she got glimpses of what looked like fairyland beyond. The surface was covered with lilies of dazzling whiteness. Scarcely a sound broke the deep and fragrant silence. Sometimes a kingfisher would rise and fly lazily away, sometimes a troop of monkeys would look down from the branches overhead and chatter, sometimes grey parrots with red tails would scream angrily for a moment at being disturbed.

But as Ma lay and enjoyed all the peace and the beauty she seemed to see other things—she saw canoe-loads of sad-eyed slaves passing down week after week, year after year, century after century—what terrible misery and despair that lovely creek must have known!

And when she landed and walked through the forest trails, the same thought was in her mind—how these paths had been beaten hard by endless files of hopeless slaves—men, women, and little children.

"At last," she said thankfully, "the cruel reign of heathendom is over, and peace and kindness and happiness are now coming to this dark land!"

She found the villages and towns almost touching one another, and full of people.

"Welcome, Ma! we looked for your coming," shouted her old friends, the slave-traders, although they knew well that she would try and stop their evil doings.

She found that some native traders from the coast had been telling the people about Jesus, and she called the chiefs and held a palaver and set about starting a school and building a church. It was curious to see not only children, but grave men and women squatting on the ground learning A B C! And some of the men were old slave-hunters.

"Come back soon, Ma! You are the only one who cares for us," they cried as she left.

One day, when coming down the Creek, she was idly watching a snake trying to swim across the quiet water, when bump, bump, her canoe was run into and nearly overturned by another, which shot out from the side.

"Sorry, Ma," said the man in it. "I have been waiting for you many days. My master at Akani Obi wants to speak with you."

The canoe was turned, and followed by the other into a creek that was fairylike in its tender beauty, and came to a beach where stood a nice-looking, well-dressed native and his wife. They took her into their home, which was furnished like a European one.

"I am Onoyom," said the man. "When I was a little slave-boy, one of your white missionaries explored as far as this. All the people fled. I was not afraid, and I took him to the chief. I was punished afterwards. When I grew up I went to the cannibal feasts at Arochuku. My master died, and ten little girls were killed and placed in his grave. I became steward of the House, and ruled as chief. My house was burned down, and my child died. I thought some enemy had done it and I wanted to murder people. I met a man who had been a teacher, and he said, 'Perhaps God is angry with you.' I said, 'I want to find this God.' He said, 'Go to the White Ma and she will help you.' I took a canoe to find you. I missed you. I left a man to wait, and he has brought you. Now, will you tell me what to do?"

As she listened Ma's eyes grew bright with joy. She talked with him and his household, telling them of Jesus and His Gospel, and praying with them, and promised to come and begin a school and church. Then they made her a cup of tea, and went with her to the beach.

As her canoe skimmed over the quiet water again, darkness fell, and a rain-storm came on and Ma was drenched, but she did not care; she sang aloud in her blitheness of heart, for after ages of darkness and wickedness the sunlight of God was beginning to shine in the Creek.

After that what a life she led! She was always moving up and down the Creek, visiting strange places and camping anywhere. Sometimes she had to sleep in the open air, or in huts on the floor, or in the canoe; sometimes she was caught in tornadoes and soaked to the skin; sometimes she was not able to wash for many days; sometimes she ran out of stores and lived on native plant-food and tea made in old milk tins. She was often ill, full of aches and pains and burning with fever; but even when she was suffering she never lost her happy spirit and her bright laugh. She was like a white spirit fluttering hither and thither, a symbol of the new life that was stirring in the land. The people were rising out of the sleep of centuries, everywhere they were eager to learn, everywhere they cried for teachers and missionaries.

"Oh," cried Ma, "if only I could do more, if only I were young again! If only the Church at home would send out scores of men and women. If . . ."

She did too much, and her frail weak body could not stand it. Sleep forsook her, and that meant loss of nerve. When she thought of the immense work opening up before her, with only herself to do it, she quailed and shrank from the task. In the night she rose and went wandering over the house, and looked down upon the children slumbering in perfect trust and peace.

"Surely, surely," she said, "God who takes care of the little ones will take care of me."

It was time for her holiday to Scotland, but she could not leave because she was very near death. A long rest revived her, and she rose—to go home? No. The flame that burned in that worn little body leapt up and glowed best in the African forest. Instead of going to Scotland she made up her mind to spend six months wandering about the Creek in her own canoe, visiting the people and opening new Mission stations.

"Oh, Ma!" said the other missionaries, "are you wise to do this after all you have gone through? You have worked so hard, and you need a holiday. Go home and rest, and then you will be better able to do what you wish."

But no, she would carry out her plan; and so giving up the Court work to be freer to serve her own Master, she set out joyfully on her quest for new toils and triumphs.

CHAPTER VIII

Ma learns to ride a bicycle and goes pioneering; the Government makes her a Judge again and she rules the people; stories of the Court, and of her last visit to Scotland with a black boy as maid-of-all-work; and something about a beautiful dream which she dreamed when she returned, and a cow and a yellow cat.

MA settled at Itu in a little mud hut, with a table and chair and a few pots and pans. The girls worked and slept anywhere; the babies, new and old crawled all over the place like caterpillars, and at night lay on bits of newspaper on the floor. Ma helped in the building of the Mission House and Church, and when they were finished sent for some one to fix up doors and windows. Mr. Chapman, from the Institution, arrived, and was treated as the guest of the people, so that when he made his bed in the middle of the church the young men of the village came, as was their custom, and slept on the floor round him as a guard of honour, and got water and food for him in the morning.

Ma was as busy as a bee. She carried on a day-school, preached to four hundred people, taught a Bible Class and a Sunday School, received visitors from dawn till dusk, and explored the forest and made friends with the shy natives. Every now and then she canoed up the Creek as far as Arochuku, and stayed in the villages along the banks. Mud-and-thatch churches began to spring up. Onoyom, however, said he was not going to be satisfied with anything less than the very best House of God, and taking three hundred pounds that he had saved up he spent it all on a fine building. When the time came to make the pulpit and seats, he said: "We want wood, cut down the juju tree." Now the juju tree is where the god of a village is supposed to live, and his men were horror-struck.

"The juju will be angry; he will not let us, he will kill us."

"Ma's God is stronger than our juju," was his reply. "Cut it down."

They went out and began the work, but the trunk was thick, and after a time they stopped.

"See, we cannot cut it."

The heathen crowd, standing in a ring watching them,

were overjoyed. "Ah, ha!" they cried, "our juju is stronger than Ma's God."

Next morning Onoyom took out a party of men who wanted to be disciples of the new faith, and before beginning to hack at the tree they knelt down and prayed that the White Mother's God would prove more powerful than the juju. Then, rising, they attacked it with lusty strokes, and soon it tottered and fell with a mighty crash. It was the turn of Onoyom to rejoice.

When the Creek churches were ready, missionaries travelled up from Calabar to open them, and were astonished to see the happy, well-clothed people, and the big sums of money they brought. At one place there was a huge pile of brass rods, the value of which was £20. You must remember that these were still heathen people, but they were longing to love and serve the true God. So eager, indeed, were they that they worried Ma until she was almost distracted. Messages came every day like this: "We want to know God: send us even a boy." "We want a White Ma like you to teach us book and washing and sewing." "We have money to pay a teacher, send one." Sometimes she laughed, and sometimes she cried.

"What can I do? I am only one poor old woman!"

Then she prayed that more missionaries might hear these calls, and come out from Scotland to help.

Sometimes another kind of cry came down the Creek. A messenger from Arochuku arrived.

"Ma, the bad chiefs are going to thrust the teachers out of the land."

Ma was startled.

"And what did the teachers say?" she asked.

"That the chiefs could put them out of the land, but they could not put them away from God."

"Good, and what do the people say?"

"That they will die for Jesus."

"Why, that is good news!" Ma exclaimed with delight. "Go and tell them to be patient and strong, and all will be well."

As there were no missionaries to come up and help her she went on alone, this time into the great dark forest-land, that stretched far to the west of Itu. It was the home of the Ibibios, that naked down-trodden race who had been so long the victims of slave-hunters, "untamed, unwashed, unlovely savages," Ma called them; but it was just because they were so wretched that she pitied them and longed to uplift them. Like Jesus, she wanted to go amongst the worst people rather than amongst the best.

The Government were now making a road through the forest, and as she looked at it stretching away so straight and level and broad, she began to dream again. "I will go with the road," she said, "and build a row of schools and churches right across the land." She had troops of friends amongst the white officers, who all admired and liked her, and they, also, urged her to come, and one said she should get a bicycle.

"Me on a bicycle!" she said. "An old woman like me!"

She had watched their bicycles going up and down the road, and was afraid of them. She said she would not go near them in case they should explode; but one of the officers brought her out a beautiful machine from England, and that cured her. She soon learned to ride, and it became a great help in her work.

One day she took Etim, another of her bright scholars, who was only twelve, and set out for a village called Ikotobong, six miles beyond Itu, in a beautiful spot amongst the hills, and started a school and congregation. Etim was the schoolmaster! And right bravely the little fellow wrought; very soon he had a hundred children deep in the first book.

The head-teacher at Ikotobong, one of those who learned to love Jesus through her, thus tells the story of her coming:

> When she walked through the town she saw many idols which we all worshipped, and she pitied us very much. Seeing that the people were sitting in darkness she asked for a dwelling-place. The town's chiefs gave her a very nice little hill in the middle of the town. And from the first day all the people were astonished very much at her wisdom, gentleness, and love, because they had never seen a white person like her before. And amazement fell upon every one in the town concerning all that she told them about God, and pleasure filled their hearts because she lived amongst them. Before she came the people hated one another, and did not sit in love and peace, but when she came to us her good influence

and love becalmed us. Though she was an old woman she had to work like a very powerful big man. The Ibibio people wondered and wondered about her in gladness, she was so full of love to every one, and working hard every day for their good. So by all her kind and compassionate work she came to be called *Adiaha Makara,* meaning the eldest daughter of all Europeans, and *Ma Akamba,* meaning great madam.

At last God answered Ma's prayers. Three things happened.

First, the Church in Scotland, which was now called the United Free Church, resolved to follow her into the wilderness and made Itu into a regular station with a doctor in charge. A hospital, called the Mary Slessor Mission Hospital, was added, and a launch was sent out for the Creek work. "It is just like a fairy-tale," said Ma. "I am so glad for the people."

Next a man missionary was sent to Arochuku, and came back with such a glowing story of the numbers of people living there, and their longing for the right way, that he was sent up at once to open a station.

Then the Church told Ma that they would place two ladies at Akpap, and she need not return, but remain in the wilds and be a pioneer.

The sky of her life, which had been so dark before, now became clear and blue and filled with sunshine.

One afternoon a Government officer visited her and said:

"Ma, what are we going to do?"

The same question was always being put to her. Everybody, from the British officials down to runaway slaves, came to her for counsel and help; few did anything in that part of the country without first talking to her about it.

"What is it now?" she asked.

"We want a magistrate for this big and important district, and we want a very clever and strong person who will be able to rule the people and see justice done."

"Well?" she asked again.

"Oh, Ma, don't you see what I'm driving at?"

"Fine that," she answered with a twinkle. "You want a very clever and strong man to rule this people, and see justice done, a very worthy aim."

"Quite so, and you are the man we want, Ma."

"Me? hoots, laddie, the tea must have gone to your head!"

"No, Ma, I'm serious. We officers can't do the work; we haven't the language for one thing, and you know it better than the natives themselves; also you know all their ways and tricks; they worship you; you have great power over them; and what a chance to protect the women and punish the men as you like! Think of the twins, Ma!"

"Ay," mused Ma, "it might help God's work. I don't like it, but I would do it for His sake."

"Thank you, Ma. Your official title will be Vice-President of the Native Court, but of course you will be the real President and do as you like. The salary will be——"

"I'll take no salary," she snapped. "I'm not doing it for the Government. I'm doing it for God."

By and by the letter from the Government came appointing her, and saying that her salary would be given to the Mission to help on her work.

So Ma became again the only woman judge in the Empire. The Court was held in a thatched building at Ikotobong. Ma sat at a small table, and around her were the chiefs getting their first lessons in acting justly and mercifully towards wrongdoers. Often she had to keep them in order. They were very fond of talking, and if they did not hold their tongues she just rose and boxed their ears.

She sat long days trying the cases, her only food a cup of tea and a biscuit and a tin of sweets. She needed all her courage to get through, for the stories of sin and cruelty and shame poured into her ears were terrible for a white woman to hear. "We do not know how she does it," the other missionaries said. She could not have done it had it not been that she wanted to save her black sisters and the little children from the misery they suffered.

She was like no other judge in the world, because she had no books to guide her in dealing with the cases, nothing but her knowledge of the laws and customs of the people and her own good sense. She knew every nook and cranny of the native mind, and although many lies are told in African Courts, no one ever deceived her. They often tried, but she always found them out, and then they would cower and slink away before her flashing eye.

Very difficult questions which puzzled the Government officials had sometimes to be decided, but Ma was never at a loss. Once two tribes laid claim to a piece of land, and a British Commissioner tried for days to find out to whom it belonged, and failed. He was in despair. Ma came, and as usual appealed to the people themselves.

"Isn't it the custom for the tribes to whom land belongs to sacrifice to it?"

"Yes, Ma."

"Can you tell the tribe that has been in the habit of sacrificing to this bit of land?"

"Yes, Ma. Our tribe," said one of the big men.

"Then it belongs to you."

"Quite right, Ma," cried every one, and they went away laughing.

The people who came to Court were so ignorant and foolish that Ma sometimes did what no other judge would do; she treated them like naughty children, and gave them a slap or a rap over the knuckles, and lectured them and sent them away. After sullen, fierce-looking men had been fined for some offence, she would take them to the Mission House and feed them and give them work. Then, in the evening, she would gather them together and talk to them about Jesus.

The oath given to the witnesses was not the British one, but the native one or *mbiam*. A pot or bottle was brought in filled with a secret liquid which had a horrible smell. One of the chiefs dipped a stick into it and put some of the stuff on the tongue, head, arm, and foot of the witnesses, who believed that if they told a lie it would kill them. They often trembled with fear when taking it. Once one died suddenly after giving false evidence, and the people thought it was a judgment upon him.

Judge Slessor had to look sharply after the native policemen, for they were important men in their own eyes, and often did things they ought not to have done. One went to summon villagers to clean the roads. The children in the Mission school were singing their morning hymn, and he rushed in among them lashing with his whip, and shouting: "Come out and clean the roads." The teachers complained, and the policeman was tried before Ma.

"You need to be punished," she said, "for you have

grown so big that you will soon be knocking your head against the roof." This pleased the people even more than the punishment he got from the jury.

The Court became famous in the land, for the people knew that Ma understood them and gave them justice. So much, indeed, did they trust her that they got into the habit of taking their quarrels and troubles first to the Mission House, and there Ma made peace and saved them going to law. Even when she was ill they came and squatted down outside her bedroom window, and the girls took in their stories to her, and she called out to the people and told them what to do.

A young man, a slave, wanted to be free, and came to Ma. "I am sorry," she said, "the Court cannot do anything, but—the country lies before you."

He took the hint, and bolted out of the district.

A huntsman, in search of game, saw a movement amongst the bushes, and cried out, "Any one there?" There was no answer, and he fired. A scream made him rush to the spot, and to his horror he found that he had shot a girl. He carried her to the nearest house, where she died. He was brought up and tried, and acquitted, as he had not meant to harm her. But native law is "life for life," and the people demanded a life for the life that had been taken. The man, in his despair, ran to Ma. Cutting off a lock of his hair, he gave it to her. This meant that all he had was hers, and that the tribe would have to deal with her too. But she knew that if he stayed he would be killed, and told him to fly, which he did.

Ma was also going on with her real work, preaching and teaching, training boys and girls to become little missionaries, and carrying the light of the Gospel further and further into the heathen forest. And, as usual, she was dreaming dreams. She now remembered the dream of Mr. Thomson to build a holiday home for the missionaries. She said to herself, "Can I not build a little one for the ladies in Calabar?" Some money came to her, and she sought out a spot on the wooded hills nearer the Creek called Use, and began to put up several mud cottages that might be used for rest-homes. She did most of the work herself, with the aid of Janie and the other girls, sleeping the while on the floor in a hut.

One night a lady missionary stayed with her who was anxious to get away early next morning.

"All right," said Ma, "I'll set the alarum clock."

The visitor looked puzzled, for there were no watches or clocks to be seen. Ma went out to the yard where the fowls were kept and brought in a rooster and tied it near the foot of her bed. At dawn the "alarum" went off; the cock crew, and the sleepers were roused.

"Ma," said a Government doctor at last, "you will die if you do not take a rest." And very sorrowfully she replied that it was likely, and so she went home to Scotland, taking Dan and leaving Janie to take care of the other children.

Dan, who was only six years old, proved a very handy little man-of-all-work. He soon learned to speak English, and ran her messages, carried her parcels, and even cooked her tit-bits of food. He had a royal time, being loaded with toys and books and sweets, and Ma was anxious that he should not be spoiled. She would often ask those with whom she stayed to allow him to sit on the floor, that he might not forget who he was.

He had quick eyes, and saw everything. When he went out in a town with Ma he begged to have the money for the street cars, for, he said, "Gentlemen always pay for the ladies!" But he did not always understand what he saw. At table he thought the sharpening of the carving-knife on the steel was part of the grace before meals!

Her friends found Ma much changed. "Oh, Mary," said one, "I didn't know you."

"Nae wonder," she said, laughing, "look at my face!" It was dark and withered and wrinkled, though her eyes were as bright and merry as ever and full of changing lights.

One day she went to pay a visit to Mrs. Scott, the lady of the manse at Bonkle, in Lanarkshire. They had written to one another for years, but had never met. There were young people there, and all were greatly excited, for the black boy was also expected. Everything that love could think of was done for the comfort of the guest. At last the cab appeared at the bend of the road, and all hurried to the gate. Down jumped Dan smiling, sure of his welcome. Then was helped out a frail and delicate lady, who looked round shyly and brightly answered all the greetings. She walked slowly up the garden path, gazing at the green lawns and the flower-beds and the borders of shady trees, and drinking in the goodness of it all.

"All this," she said, "and for me!"

She was so weak and ill that she was glad to sink into a cushiony chair placed for her in the sunniest corner of the sunny room. The young girls followed her in. Stretching out her hands towards them, she cried:

"Oh! how many of you lassies am I to get?"

And, glad to tell, she did get one, Miss Young, who went out to Calabar and became to her like a daughter, and was afterwards picked out by the Church as the one best fitted to carry on the work that lay closest to her heart after she herself was done with it all.

It was times like these that made Ma young again. She just wandered quietly about in the woods and meadows, or went and listened to the music practices in the church. She was delighted with the singing, and before leaving thanked the precentor for the pleasure she had got, and he gave her his tuning-fork, which he valued, and she kept it as one of her treasures to the end.

Coming out one night after the service, she looked up to the starry sky, and said, "These stars are shining upon my bairns—I wonder how they are"; and once, when "*Peace, perfect peace? with loved ones far away!*" was sung, she said: "I was thinking all the time of my children out there."

She missed them more and more as the months went on. One afternoon, when she was sitting down to tea in a house in Perthshire, she begged to be allowed to hold a red-cheeked baby-boy on her knee. "It is more homely," she said, "and I have been so used to them all these years."

Then she made up her mind. "I cannot stay longer, I am growing anxious about my children. I am sure they need me." Her friends tried to keep her, but no, she must go. They bade her farewell at one or two large meetings, where her figure, little and fragile, and worn by long toil in the African sun, brought tears to many eyes. The meetings were very solemn ones. As she spoke of the needs of Africa, one who listened said: "It is not Mary Slessor who is speaking, but God."

One night before she sailed she was found crying quietly

in bed, not because she had no friends, for she had many, but because all her own loved ones were dead, and she was homeless and lonesome. She just wanted her mother to take her into her arms, pat her cheek, and murmur, as she had done long ago, " Good-bye, lassie, and God be with you."

Dan did not wish to leave all the delights of his life in Scotland, and although he had mechanical toys and books and sweets to cheer him, he sobbed himself to sleep in the train.

So Ma looked her last upon the dear red and grey roofs and green hills of Scotland, for she never saw them again.

She went to Use, which now became her home. It was a lonely place amongst trees, near the great new highway. A wonderful road that was. Bordered by giant cotton trees and palms, it ran up and down, over the hills, without touching a village or town. These were all cleverly hidden away in the forest, for the people had not got over their terror of the slave-hunters. Except on market-days the road was very silent, and you met no children on it, for they were afraid of being seized and made slaves. Leopards and wild cats roamed over it at night.

At one part a number of rough concrete steps led to the top of the steep bank, from which a narrow path wound up the hillside and ended in a clearing in the bush. Here stood Ma's queer patchwork mud-house, just a shapeless huddle of odd rooms, with a closed-in verandah, the whole covered with sheets of trade-iron, tin from mission-boxes, and lead from tea-chests. It was hard to find the door, the steps of which were of unhewn stones.

She began to work harder than ever. What a wonder she was! She did all the tiresome Court business, sometimes sitting eight hours patiently listening to the evidence; she held palavers with chiefs; she went long journeys on foot into the wilderness, going where no white man went. On Sundays she visited and preached at ten or twelve villages, and between times she was toiling about the house, making and mending, nailing up roofs, sawing boards, cutting bush, mudding walls, laying cement. Was it surprising that her hands were rough and hard, and often sore and bleeding?

She was seldom well, and always tired, so tired that at night she was not able to take off her clothes, and lay down with them on until she slept a little and was rested, and then she rose and undressed. At times she was on the point of fainting from pain, and only got relief from sleeping-draughts. It was true of her what one of the missionaries said: "God does most of His work here by bodies half-dead, but alive in Christ."

She had now, however, hosts of friends, all willing to look after her. Nearly every one, officials, missionaries, traders, and natives, were kind to her. Sir Walter Egerton, the British Governor, and Lady Egerton would send her cases of milk for the children, and the officials pressed upon her the use of their steamers and motor-cars and messengers and workmen. At Ikotobong was Miss Peacock, that girl with the great thoughtful eyes who had listened so eagerly to Ma when she had addressed the class in Falkirk years before. She became one of the many white daughters who hovered about her in the last years and ministered to her. Two missionary homes were open to her in Calabar, those of Mr. and Mrs. Wilkie and Mr. and Mrs. Macgregor, and there she was always made comfortable and happy.

Once Government officials found her so ill that they lifted her into the motor-car and took her down to the Mission House at Itu. Something rare and precious was there, a bonnie white child, the daughter of the doctor missionary. During the first few days when Ma was fighting for her life, little Mamie often went to her side and just stood and stroked her hand for a while, and then stole quietly away.

When the turn for the better came, she charmed Ma back to health by her winning ways. For hours they swung together in the hammock on the verandah, and laughed and talked and read, their two heads bent over the pages of *Chatterbox* and *The Adviser*, and over the *Hippopotamus Book* and *Puddleduck*, and other entrancing stories. Sometimes they got so absorbed in these that time was forgotten, and "Oh, bother!" they said when the sound of the gong called them to meals. Ma was still a little child at heart.

After she returned to Use a new church was opened at Itu, and as she was not able to go down she wrote this letter to Mamie:

I may not get to the big function, which will make me rather cross, as I have looked forward to it. Anyhow if I am not there will you pop my collection into the plate for me, like a bonnie lassie ? I wish it were multiplied by ten.

I wanted you and me to have a loan of that pretty picture-book of your mother's. It has all the blouses and hats and togs that they keep in the store in Edinburgh, and I was just set on our sitting together and picking out a nice coat and hat and pinafore, all of our own choosing, for you to wear in Scotland. Oh! but you may be going to England ? Oh well, they are much the same. But here we can't do it, for it will be too late to get them for you to land in. Anyhow ask that dear Mummy of yours to help you to choose, and you will buy them with these "filthy lucre" pennies. Mind, the Bible calls them "filthy lucre," so I am not saying bad words!

Now, dear wee blue eyes, my bonnie birdie, are we never to have a play again or a snuggly snug ? We shall see, but I shall never forget those days with old Brown and Mittens and the Puddleduck relations, and all your gentle ways and winsome plays. Be Mama's good lassie and help her with all the opening day's work, and you yourself will be the bonniest there. If I am there you will sit beside me!

Ma's mind was as restless as her body. She was for ever planning what more she could do for Jesus. Her new dream was a beautiful one, perhaps the best of all. To understand it you must know that the women and girls in West Africa all belonged to households, and were bound, by native law, to obey the heads of these—their masters. The compounds were their only homes. If they became Christians they still had to do what their heathen masters told them. When they were given orders which as true servants of Jesus they could not obey without doing wrong, they were in a fix, for if they left the compounds it was not easy for them to live, as they had no houses in which to stay and no farms where they could work and grow food. Ma had often thought of the problem, and now she made up her mind that the women and girls must be taught simple trades, so that if they had to leave the compounds they would be able to support themselves.

And this was her dream. She would start a home for women and girls where she would take in waifs and refugees and other helpless ones, and train them to do things, such as the weaving of baskets, the making of bamboo furniture, shoe-making, and so on. They could also rear fowls and goats and cows, and dig, and grow food-plants and fruit-trees. And best of all, they would learn to be clean and tidy and womanly.

Ma was never long in making her dreams begin to take form. She went out one morning to look round the land at Use. Why, Use was the very place for the settlement! She would begin in a small way with just a few cottages and a garden, and gradually make it bigger. She started at once, and soon had many useful trees and plants in the ground, and fowls and goats and a cow in the yard.

That cow was a wild one, and a great bother, as it was always breaking out and wandering into the forest. Ma had no tinkling bell, but she tied a tin pail to the beast so that the rattling noise might tell where it was.

The stock had to be watched, for wild animals roamed about after dark, and leopards often sprang into the yard in search of prey.

One or two rooms at Use were kept for visitors. The doors of these were sealed up with strips of bamboo and mud until they were wanted. Once two lady missionaries arrived, and had to sleep a night before the doors were hung. Not long before a leopard had carried off the cow's calf, and the ladies thought it wise to barricade the hole. Ma looked on smiling, and said:

"There will be rats and lizards and centipedes, and maybe a snake, but a leopard would never come in . . . even though it did it would just look at you and go away again."

"We'll not give it the chance, Ma," said the ladies.

"Well, I'll give you the cat: it will scare the rats at any rate."

This cat, a big yellow one, had been found, when a kitten meowing piteously by the side of a bush track, and was taken to the Mission House, where it became a favourite with Ma. It always travelled with her, lying in a canvas bag at the bottom of the canoe, or motor-car, and sometimes she carried it on her shoulder.

The night did turn out to be a lively one, for although no leopard came, every other kind of creeping and jumping and flying thing paid the ladies a visit, and there was not much rest for them, nor for the yellow cat, which hunted the rats until the dawn.

CHAPTER IX

Ma goes farther up the Creek and settles in a heathen town in the wilds; she enters into happy friendships with young people in Scotland; has a holiday in a beautiful island, where she makes a secret compact with a lame boy; and is given a Royal Cross for the heroic work she has done.

ONE day there came out of the unknown a black boy with a number of strange-looking men.

"Mökömö Ma," he said, "I salute you. We come to see you. We are from Ikpe. The soldiers and the people fought there and the people fled. I know about you and I told them and they want your help."

"Ikpe?" echoed Ma. "Where is that? I never heard of it."

"Far up the Creek," he replied vaguely; "two days by canoe. A big town."

"But I never knew of trading canoes going there."

"No, Ma they don't allow Calabar men at Ikpe."

'Oh, I see, a closed market. Well, what do they wish?"

"They want to be god-men and learn book."

She talked long with the men, whose cry was: "Come yourself, Ma, come back with us."

It was known that she was always ready to go anywhere at a moment's notice.

"No, not now, I cannot, but I'll come soon"; and having her promise they went away with light hearts.

She was growing very, very feeble, and she shrank from entering a new place, where she would have no friends amongst the natives and could see no white faces, but the spirit of adventure still tugged at her heart, and one morning she boarded a canoe and went up the river.

It was a wonderful thing, even for her, to lie in the canoe and watch the changing beauty of the Creek. They passed the places she knew, and then came to a region that was strange to her. Hour after hour they sped, pushing through the tangle of water-lilies, watching the fishermen plunging their spears into the mud after fish, passing farms where the green corn was sprouting, and bare landing-beaches where long canoes lay side by side, coasting along stretches of thick jungle where the water was green and the air cool; where lovely flowers and ferns grew on the branches, and monkeys gambolled and swung by their tails; where butterflies and dragon-flies glinted in the sunlight, and snakes slid down old trunks and stole rustling away.

Now and again she saw the snout of a hippopotamus, with its beadlike eyes, watching them, and noted that the banks were scored by their massive feet. After they had done eight hours' paddling one of these monsters rose angrily in front and opened its enormous jaws as if it would swallow the canoe and the paddlers and Ma and all. The stream was narrow and darkness was falling, and Ma said, "Well, well, old hippo, we won't dispute your right to turn us aside." The canoe made for the bank, and Ma stayed all night in a dirty little hut swarming with mosquitoes. The chief here had heard of her and the Jesus religion, and was already praying to what was to him the unknown God. "And my people just laugh at me," he said. Ma prayed with him and cheered him and left him happier.

In the lovely morning light the canoe went on, until the Creek became like one of these little streams which feed the mills in Scotland. Ma had at last to get out and walk through the bush. She came to Ikpe, a large mud town, very dirty and smelly, where all sorts of tribes mingled, and found that the people wore little or no clothes, that the girls and boys ran about naked, and that all, old and young, seemed more wicked and shameless than any natives she had seen.

Only a few welcomed her, and these, having heard of her promise, and knowing that she always kept her word, had begun to build a church, with two rooms at the end for her to live in. It was situated in a circle of tall palm trees, among which monkeys romped and chattered.

She remained some days, living on native food, and when she left told the people she would come back.

Several times she returned, and always the people asked:

"Ma, have you come to stay?"

"No, not yet."

"Oh, Ma, when are you coming?"

What could she reply? How could she leave the work at Use? She begged the Church to send up other ladies, but the months passed, and meanwhile two churches were ready in the district, and the people were beseeching her to come.

"It's another call," she said, "and I must obey. I'm an old woman and not very fit, but I'll do my best, and I'll carry on the work at Use too. No more idleness for me!"

So up and down the Creek she went. The journey always took the best part of two days. A canoe, with ten paddlers, was sent down from Ikpe to the beach near Itu. What a bustle there was at Use before everything was ready! Then the house had to be shut up. This was done by nailing the windows, and building in the doorways with strips of wood and clay.

In the afternoon the household set off, Ma sitting in the centre of the canoe on a chair, and the children and babies round her, and the yellow cat in its bag at her feet. When it grew dark they landed at some village and spent the night, and before daybreak at four o'clock they were off again. Ma did not like the bit which was haunted by hippos. "But," she would say, "they haven't touched me yet, they just push up their ugly heads and stare at me."

When the sun became strong and they were all hot and tired they went ashore at a clearing, and the paddlers lit a fire and cooked some food, Ma joking all the time to keep everybody happy. Ikpe beach was reached about four in the afternoon, and there was still a long walk before them, and it was a very weary company that lay down to rest.

The paddlers were just the wild boys of Ikpe, very good-hearted under all their badness, as Ma told the Sunday School children of Wellington Church, Glasgow:

> They are ungrudging hard workers too. They paddle the whole day, singing as merrily as if the sun were not beating on them like a blazing fire. When we came up a month ago we had such a heavy load of timber for building purposes that they could hardly get a seat. One chief on the road asked me to put a part of it at his beach as they would never be able to take it up, but the boys sturdily answered, "The canoe is good, let us go on."
>
> They pulled eight hours on end without stopping to eat a bite. About seven o'clock we all lay down, after holding worship in the canoe, and didn't they sing! And then the moon began to show through the mist about 3 A.M., and they jumped

and pushed off, and then for eight hours pulled and sang and laughed and shouted in their high spirits, wakening the echoes of dreadful-looking places, where mud and ooze hold the crocodile and other creatures.

It was the same coming back, and when they all arrived at Use they broke a little hole in the doorway and crept in and threw themselves down on bed and floor until morning. They were often soaked, and Ma sometimes was so tired and ill and racked with pain that she could not leave the canoe, but slept in it all night. "However can you do it?" she was asked. "Oh," she replied cheerily, "I just take a big dose of medicine and wrap myself in a blanket and manage fine."

Once when she got back to Use she found that a tornado had damaged the house, and she began to repair it with her own hands. The hard work was too much for her, and she took to her bed and became delirious. Yet she struggled up and went over to the church and sat in a chair and preached.

A young missionary, Dr. Hitchcock, had come out to take charge of the medical station at Itu for a time. He had heard of Ma and of her masterful ways, but he was strong too, and not afraid of her, and when he saw her so ill he took her in charge and ordered her firmly to do what he bade her, just as if she had been a child. Poor Ma! She was a child in strength then, and she obeyed him meekly, and he treated her like a mother and she loved him as a son, and under his kind and watchful care she gradually got better. "But you mustn't cycle any more," he said, "you are past that now." So some friends in Scotland sent her out a basket-chair on wheels which the boys and girls pushed, and in this she continued to make her journeys into the forest.

A special joy in these lonely days was the love of many girls and boys at home. She told one that she had always a few choice packets of letters lying beside her chair and bed, and took them up as one would take up a book, and read them over and over again. Many were from her little friends. They told her about their schools, their games, their holidays, their pets, and their books—the letters of one boy, she said, were always like a sardine tin, they were so packed full of news—and she sent long replies back, wonderful replies, full of fun and stories and nonsense and good sense.

One of the mothers said she was very kind to take such bother.

"Why," she wrote, "look at their kindness to me! The darlings, with their perfectly natural stories and their ways of looking at everything out of a child's clear innocent eyes, and the bubbling over of the joys of a healthy life. It is a splendid tonic, and just a holiday to me too, taking me with them to the fields and the picnics and the sails on the lochs. Oh, one can almost feel the cool breeze and hear their shouts. Don't you think for a moment that though I am like a piece of wrinkled parchment my heart is not as young as ever it was, and that I don't prefer children to grown-up folks a thousand times over. I would need to, for they have been my almost sole companions for twenty-five years back. Oh, the girls at home are so bonnie with their colour and their hair and their winsome ways. I just loved to look at and to talk with them when I could. In church and Sunday School they were a thing of beauty and a joy to me all the time. I don't say that I don't love black bairns better and know them better than white ones, for I do. But one must confess to the loveliness of Scottish girls."

One of her most loving and diligent little correspondents was Christine Grant Millar Orr, who stayed in Edinburgh, and was, at this time, just thirteen, a clever girl, fond of writing stories and poems, and as good as she was clever.

Her fresh young heart went out to the weary and lonely old lady in the African bush who chatted to her so charmingly. "You have a genius for letter-writing," she told Ma. "Your letters are so full of news and yet so full of love and tenderness and your own dear self."

Here is a bit from one of Ma's letters to her:

What a bonnie morning this is! It will be dark and cold with you. It is half-past six, and I am in the little verandah which is my sanctum. We have had breakfast, but I am not yet able to do any work, as I need an hour or so to get the steam up. So I shall bid you a good-morning, and just wish you could be here to enjoy our bush, and cocoa-nut and oil and wine palms which surround us, all wrapped in a bewitching lovely blue haze from the smoke of the wood fire. Yes, you would even enjoy the pungent smell of the bush smoke, and would think there were few places like Calabar. . . But an hour later! Oh, it *will* be hot!

Ma thus tells Christine about the "smokes" season, which lasts from November to February:

It is a funny season when the air is so thick with what seems fine sand that you can't see ten yards away, and the throat and back of the nose and the whole head is dry and disagreeable, just like influenza at home. Between these "smokes," which are supposed to come from the Great Sahara Desert, the hot season blazes forth in all its fury and one feels so languid and feeble, and wonders where one can go for a breath of air or a mouthful of cold water. Then the snow on the moors and the biting winds and the sea waves of your cold land sing their siren songs.

No wonder Christine wrote back:

How I should love to take you bodily out of African heat and work and give you a long sweet holiday at The Croft, with your face to the greenest field in Scotland, and the great hills and the fresh caller air everywhere. The blossom, white and pink, the laburnum, the heavy masses of hawthorn, the sweet odours of wallflower, the calling of the blackbirds, the mossy lawn, the shady glade with birch trees and wild hyacinths and baby birdies in the hedges, and the glorious warm spring sunshine gliding through the leaves—how you would love them all!

Kind hearts at home knew of the longing for a change that sometimes came to Ma, and one of the ladies of the Church, Miss Cook, like a fairy godmother, quietly arranged that she should take a trip to the Canary Islands, and paid all the cost. Ma felt it was a very selfish thing for her to accept when there were others who also needed a rest, but the doctors said:

"Ma, if you go you will be able for a lot of work yet."

"In that case," she replied, "I'll go." She took Janie with her.

It was her first real holiday, for she had nothing to do but bask in the sunshine among the flowers and be petted by everybody, especially by Mr. and Mrs. Edisbury, who managed the hotel at which she stayed. What a time of joy it was! "From the first hour we arrived in fear and trembling," she said, "to the hour we left with a heart full to overflowing, our visit was a delicious vision of every kind of loveliness."

She was not long in the hotel before she heard that Mrs. Edisbury had a little lame son, nine years old, named Ratcliffe, who could only walk about on crutches. She could hardly walk herself then, and her tender heart was filled with love and pity and sympathy for the boy. "Oh," she said, "I must see him." She found him in the nursery, a very bright and eager child, and at once they became fast friends. For hours he would sit by her side, his great grey-blue eyes fixed on her face, while she told him thrilling stories of her adventures in wild Africa.

Before they parted they had a quiet talk and made a secret bargain. Each was to do something every day only known to themselves; nobody was to be told—not even Ratcliffe's own mother. His face was glowing when they were planning it, and he felt it was splendid to have a secret which one would think about from day to day, but which no other person would know of. His mother and aunt heard that it had been made, and sometimes they teased him to tell, but he just smiled, and nothing ever made him open his lips and speak of it. We shall learn by and by what it was.

On board the steamer going back Ma wrote a long letter to Ratcliffe:

You were in the land of Nod long before our boat came in, so neither Janie nor myself could go to say good-bye to you. But what do you think your dear daddy did? Just came away with us in the middle of the night, in the dark and the cold, and took us to the boat with all our luggage and stuff, and in the dark found our way for us to the big steamer, and then up the long stair at the ship's side, and brought us into the cabin where I am now sitting, and which has to be our home for the next ten days or so. And your dear mother waited up to say good-bye, and so did your dear aunty, and they sent us off laden with apples and flowers, and, better still, with warm loving wishes and hopes that we should meet again. My heart was glad and thankful, but it was very sore and sorry, and I am afraid I cried a wee bit when Mr. Edisbury went away out into the dark and left us. How happy your dear parents and your auntie made us! and how good it was to meet you. It will ever live as a picture in my heart and memory the times we spent with you, and it was very good for Janie to know you. . . .

We have a crowd on board, and to-day we had a birthday cake to tea, because it is a lady's birthday. As no one ever asks a lady how old she is—you remember us talking about that—well, they put 21 on the icing of the cake, but she is an old lady, and they made her funny presents, a little dolly, and a china pug dog with a tail that keeps wagging after you have touched it, and some beads. It was such fun. There is so little to do on board that every one gets wearied, and wants a bit of fun to pass the hours away. . . .

And now, dear little friend, good-bye. Be good and brave, and hurry putting your pennies in the bank so that you can come to see us and stay a long time. Janie sends her compliments to you and to all, and says, " Do not forget us." So say I.

Joyful days in Ratcliffe's life were these when letters arrived from Ma, " bang, bang from the wilds," as she said. In all she spoke of the mysterious secret. " Now, sonny," she would say, " do you remember our little secret treaty? I do, and keep it. There is a telephone and a telegraph, secret, wireless, swift, which never fails, and it carries to Canary *via* the Kingdom of God." Or this, " Are you remembering our old secret? Dear old sweetheart, so am I, and I get surer and surer than ever for the BEST. Keep on! "

Sometimes Ratcliffe wrote in reply, sometimes his mother or auntie, but always there was a message to say that " the secret was being kept."

Ratcliffe liked to hear about the children and their doings and about the teeming life of the forest, " cunning things among insects and beautiful flies and butterflies and small creatures among the bushes glistening like fine stones or flowers," but best of all he loved the snake stories like this:

One night in the dark there came up to my ears small screams from below. Janie was jumping about and Annie and she were throwing things, and by the light of the fire it looked awful. Janie laughed back to my screams, " It is a snake, don't come," and she was lashing all she was able with a stick. Annie was making noise, and not much more. I got round in my slow way to the outside. Janie had forced it back till she and Annie and Maggie were all on the outside and could run, but Janie held on, and I threw her a machete and she hacked the thing into bits. In the morning the bits were all gone, some other beast had eaten it, and there were only marks. Another day Janie was chasing with the others a horrid thing we call Asawuri. I don't know what it is in scientific English. It makes a long oo-o-oo-o of a note and lives in the bush in a hole. It is bigger than a lizard and marked handsomely like a snake, and has a deadly poison ; that's why God has given it the note of warning, I suppose. Janie killed it. . . . I am always keeping my secret. Are you ? Don't slacken ! Don't tell.

Ma always tried to cheer and help him :

I expect you will be at school by this time. Are you? How do you like it ? Do the masters give any punishments ? I am sure they won't need to do that with you, for you will be doing your best. But it will sometimes be hard to do lessons when it is hot, and you will want to do other things ; and let me whisper a secret to you. I, too, am an awful duffer at arithmetic ! I simply can't do it. Never mind, I've got on fairly well, and so will you ; and now I have only the sums of the boys in the school to bother me, and I never give them harder ones than I can do quickly and explain well myself. You will come out on top some day. All the same, try for all you are worth and catch up. Auntie and mother will help you—that's what aunties and mothers are for, you know. Just you put your arms round auntie's neck and look at her with your bonnie speaking eyes, and you'll see what will happen. Janie can't count at all, she never could, and I had a great pity always for her, and yet what could I do without Janie ? She is worth a thousand mathematicians to me and to our people.

Ma rejoiced that she was able to do a little more for her beloved Master, and she began to take more care of her health. She did not want to be great or famous, only to walk very quietly from day to day, and do simple things, looking after the needs of her people and fighting the sin and ignorance that marred their lives. So we find her again at Use and Ikpe spending the long hours preaching, teaching, doctoring, building, cementing, painting, varnishing—a very humble and happy woman.

She paid a visit to Okoyong, the first since she had left eight years before. The wild old station had become so quiet and peaceful that it was almost like a bit of Scotland, and there was a fine new church. Everybody came to " köm " her, and she could scarcely get her meals for talking about the long ago. She saw Eme Ete and Mana, and Iye the mother of Susie, and Esien, now a leading Christian, and many others ; and when she went over to the church she found four hundred people gathered to hear her, the men and boys in the centre, and the women in coloured frocks and head-dresses at the side, while the children sat in rows on the floor. All were clean and tidy, and she thought what a big change it was from the terrible days when the naked villagers were only fond of drink and bloodshed.

"Yes," said a church member later to one of the lady missionaries, "even the leopards became less bold and dangerous when Ma came!"

She was glad to have a talk with Eme Ete, but sorry to know that she was still a heathen, and sacrificed every day in her yard to a mud white-washed figure of a woman that had egg-shells for eyes. There was also a mud altar on which she laid her offerings of palm-wine, gin, and food, and sometimes she put a fowl or eggs in the lap of the image. Her rooms were full of charms, such as bunches of grass and feathers and bottles. It made Ma very sad. Eme Ete died soon after, and from the roof of her house was hung a great fold of white satin, which is a sign of death in a heathen home, and the doors were shut and the place left to rot and fall to pieces.

Though Ma was hidden away in the African forest and thought she was a nobody, there were others who, knowing what she had done, and having been helped by her example, made up their minds that her story should not be left untold. They wrote it out, and by and by it came into the hands of Sir Frederick Lugard, the Governor-General of Nigeria, as the whole country was now called, and he, marvelling at the tale, sent it home so that it might be brought to Royal notice.

One day a native runner appeared in the yard at Use with a bundle of letters, amongst which was a large one that looked important. Ma turned it over and wondered what it could be. It was from a very famous and ancient society, the Order of the Hospital of St. John of Jerusalem, which has the King at its head and other Royal persons amongst its officials, begging that she would agree to become one of its Honorary Associates and accept the Silver Cross which it gave to those who were noted for goodness and good work.

She looked at her torn dress and her rough hands and her

bare feet, and around at the poor little shanty of a house, and chuckled.

"Fancy me with a Royal medal!" she said. "What have I done? I dinna deserve anything for doing my duty. I couldna' even have done that unless God had been with me all the time. To Him be all the honour."

"But," she added, "it's nice too, for it will let the folk here ken that the King is interested in the work that we are doing." And so, being a loyal subject, she wrote back, saying "Yes."

Another letter arrived telling her that her election had been approved by King George V., and then came the beautiful diploma. But she had to go down to Duke Town to be given the Cross at a public meeting, and this was a great trial. Everybody, however, was kind and treated her like a princess. While they were praising her she sat with her face buried in her hands, and when she spoke she made it seem as if the honour were done to the Mission and not to herself. A bouquet of roses was handed to her, and when she got home to Use she planted a stem beside the rough-hewn steps, and to her delight it grew and flourished. When she died a cutting from it was planted on her grave.

Of course she had to tell Ratcliffe all about the affair. "The Silver Cross," she said, "is a nice thing called a decoration, which one wears on special occasions, and is just like a prize given at school to a boy. You wonder what I got a prize for? So do I! I can't make it out at all. But you see our King is so good and kind, he is always doing nice things, and this is one of them."

Ashamed of all that people were saying and writing about her, she hastened up to Use, where she pinned the cross on her breast to show the girls how it looked.

By this time Mary and Annie were married and had homes of their own, and Alice and Maggie were at Duke Town learning to wash and iron and cut out and make clothes, and Dan was also at school. Once Dan had a splendid holiday, and Ma tells Ratcliffe about it:

Dan has gone up the Cross River with his master to a new country where coal has been found and where tin has been found, and where our wonderful fellow-countrymen are to build a railway which will enter and open up new lands and peoples and treasures, and add to the wealth and greatness of our Empire. The coal will make the biggest changes you can think of. It is like a fairy tale. Just think, if we have coal, we can start to manufacture everything out here, for we have material for almost everything, and all the timber in these endless forests can then be sent over the world. And what crowds of people from Britain and here will be getting employment at the railways and the mines! It is a wonderful old world this, isn't it? We are always hearing that it is played out.

Among the men who were opening up the wild country, officials, engineers, and traders, Ma had many dear friends, and she was always praising them up for the work they were doing.

"We come of a wonderful race, Ratcliffe," she said. "How proud I am of our countrymen many a time. How brave they are! What knowledge and grit they possess! How doggedly they hold on! How they persevere and win! No wonder a handful of them rule the horde of natives and leave their mark. The native, clever in his own way, just stares and obeys."

CHAPTER X

This chapter tells how Ma became a gipsy again and lived on a hill-top, and how after a hard fight she won a new region for Jesus; gives some notes from her diary and letters to little friends at home, and pictures her amongst her treasures.

SOME distance from Ikpe there is a high hill called Odoro Ikpe, on which the Government has a rest-house.

Ma climbed up there one Saturday night.

"What a grand view!" she cried, as she looked over the wide plain and breathed in the cool fresh wind with a great content, "I've never been so high before."

And then her eyes grew sad. For all that green country was the home of heathenism. The chiefs had shut and bolted the door of their hearts against Jesus, and would not let any teachers or missionaries come in and disturb their ways.

Ma had often gone to them in her wheeled chair, fording rivers, crossing swamps, pushing through wet forests, and stood and knocked at their hearts in His name, but in vain. They were afraid that if she came all their old fashions would tumble down about their ears.

She was not the one to lose courage. As she sat there on the hill-top, she dreamed that she saw the whole region being won for Jesus, and the people coming to His house clothed and in their right mind.

"O God!" she prayed, "old and feeble and unworthy as I am, help me to win them."

And there and then she put on her armour and braced herself for battle

"Janie," she said, "we'll stay here until we overcome these chiefs."

Janie looked round and grunted. The rest-house had only holes for windows; there was a doorway, but no door; the floor was of dried mud, and there was not even a table or a chair. But Ma could be happy with nothing, she would have been content with bare ground for a bed, and the starry sky for a covering. She did, indeed, find that it was better to sleep in the open air than in the stuffy rest-house, and she lay down every night in the verandah with the cool wind fanning her cheeks.

Day after day she called the chiefs and talked with them; she coaxed the little boys and girls, who were timid and sullen, to come and learn A B C; she stood at night in the villages when the women were cooking at their fires and the young people were dancing to the sound of the drum, and spoke to all who would listen of the love of Jesus and His power to free them from sin.

And at last, after a weary struggle, her patience and goodness and humour melted the hard hearts, and one by one the chiefs came and said they would allow her to do anything she liked, and they would try to worship her God and learn the new ways.

Her heart was full. She went out in the cool of the night and stood gazing over the dim plain. All was silent and still, and the stars were shining more gloriously than she had ever seen them before. Her eyes swept over them, as they often did, and rested on the Southern Cross, the group she loved most of all, because it was the symbol of her dear Lord watching over the dark and sinful world, and her thin worn face was beautiful, for her dream had come true.

She went in and sat on the floor, and leant her weary back against the wall of the room, and wrote by the light of a candle stuck in its own grease, telling her friends how happy she was—the happiest woman in all the world.

"I can't think," she said, "why God has so highly honoured and trusted me."

She was a wreck, her body was a mass of pain, she was growing deaf and blind, she was tired and weak, and oh, so lonely! Yet her heart was bursting with love and gratitude and joy. O wonderful Ma!

All this time she was working three stations—Use, Ikpe, and Odoro Ikpe, and going constantly between them. She kept a diary, and every night—often in the middle of the night—she wrote in it the story of the day. And what a story of toil and heroism it is! Here are one or two little sentences from it:

Left the beach for Ikpe in the evening, sail in moonlight; reached Ikpe 4 P.M. next day; ran on to a tree; boys thrown into the water.

Egbo out all night, screaming and drumming like madmen till daylight. All drunk.

First night in new house. Sorry to leave the wee hut I have enjoyed so much comfort and blessing in.

Patients from early morning; man bitten by rat; another by snake. School begun, nearly a hundred scholars.

First Christian funeral at Ikpe.

Chiefs here by daybreak for palavers.

Splendid congregation. People changing for the better.

Terrific thunderstorm. School-boys drenched. Got a big fire on in hall, and all sat round the blaze and I gave them a reading lesson.

A great reception at Use—thank God for the girls and home. Thank God for sleep!

On roof all day, head and neck aching, hands broken and bleeding.

Carrying sand, cleaning corn patch, mudding and rubbing walls.

Cut my first two roses from the rose bush—lovely, a tender gift from God.

After sleepless night found white ants in millions in the drawers.

Washed a big washing.
Terrific rain storm, no school.
Very feeble, scarcely able to stand upright in church.
Horrid night with cross child.
Lovely letters from dear ones. God is very good to me.
Every boy in school clothed to-day for first time.
Heaps of sick babies.
Full up with work till late at night. Dead tired.
Two women murdered on the way from market and their heads taken away.
Fever; trying to make a meat safe.
Sleepless night, baby screaming every few minutes.
Splendid fever-sleep full of dreams. Thank God for daily strength to go on however feeble. Thank God for the girls who got up and got me tea without any bother.
Reached Rest House at darkening. A fearful night of misery with mosquitoes, and hard filthy ground on which we lay. Rose at first streak of dawn and never was so glad to leave a place. Baby yelled all night.
Nothing done, low fever, but a very happy day.
Fever, stupor sleep. Lost count of days.
Useless after utterly sleepless night. Made such sermons and delivered them all night long.

Her friends in Scotland began to call her home, tempting her with visions of rest and peace and lazy days in gardens amongst flowers and all sorts of good and loving things, but though she thought of it with longing and tears, she said she must first build a house on the hill-top of Odoro Ikpe to be ready for a missionary when the Church sent one. After that perhaps . . .

So she started to put up her last house, and because she was so feeble and her gang of labourers were such idlers and drones, she found it the hardest task she had ever tried to do. " The African works well," she said, " if you are at hand to guide and spur him on, but just leave him and he sits down and talks or sleeps till you come back." So vexed sometimes was she with the men dawdling over their trifling bit of work that she would rise and box their ears, but they just laughed and thought it a fine joke. Ma did not like to do such things: she wrote to one of her little correspondents: " You would have thought your missionary friend was rather hard-hearted, but hard things have to be done and said when one's heart aches to say and do most melting things."

Ma had more hope of the children than of the grown-ups, and she tried to get hold of them and teach them. "Though they are black," she told a boy in the Highlands, "they are just as bonnie and nice as if they were white. Indeed the colour does not matter. We are all the same inside our heads and hearts, and the little lads who know about Jesus are trying as hard to be good and brave Christians as you boys who are white."

She was specially hopeful about the boys. Once a missionary spoke to her about one who seemed to have no wish to be a Christian, and she replied, "Dinna gie up hope. You dinna ken what is behind him and what he has to fight against. His mother has maybe made him promise not to do it—perhaps made him chop *mbiam* (take the solemn oath) over it." And after she talked with the boy she said, "He's a fine laddie, and ye'll have him yet."

Many boys came to her for help in their troubles, and how patiently she listened to what they had to say, and how wisely and tenderly she spoke to them! She loved them all, and thought about them just as a kind mother would have done. To those who were going to be taught and trained she said, "You must be the leaders of your race and help them to rise, but you can only lead others to Jesus if you follow Him closely yourself."

That was always what she was telling her own children: "Keep close to Jesus." "Bairns," she would say, "it's the wee lassie that sits beside her mother at meal-times that gets all the nice bittocks. The one who sits far away and sulks disna ken what she misses. Even the pussy gets more than she does. Keep close to Jesus the Good Shepherd all the way."

When the Government took a number of the Ikpe lads to work on the new railway being built to the coal-fields they came to Ma and said they were afraid to go so far.

"God will go with you and keep you," she said. "Try and find out some one who preaches the Gospel and keep near him."

On the fly-leaf of a Bible she gave one of them, she wrote:

Udō Ekpenyoñ Edikpo.

Trusting he will hold by the truths of this Holy Book when in the midst of strangers he may be exposed to temptation. Never forget prayer when reading.—Your friend,

M. SLESSOR.

"This book," she told Udö, "will be a lamp to you and guide you."

These young men returned none the worse of their exile.

The boys who wanted to be good had more to put up with than those at home. At Ikpe there was an *mbre*, or play, called *ekang*, and all young men had to join it and pay a fee of £10. Those who would not were fined ten rods, some fish, some leaves called *akan*, and two jars of palm wine, and had to appear in the street and dance backwards to the beat of the drum, and then were flogged and hounded to their homes. This custom Ma put down.

Once the chiefs gave orders that all men were to hunt in the bush, and the animals caught were to be sacrificed and eaten in honour of the *Ndems* in the town. The lads of the Church refused to go to the hunt or to eat of the sacrifice. "Then," said the chiefs, "you will be banished." Word was sent to Ma, who was at Use, and when she came she told the chiefs that no lad must be forced to do anything against his conscience, and from that day to this there has been neither hunt nor sacrifice.

The people sacrificed and ate animals before the *Ndems*, because they believed that it would make the yams on their farms grow big. Ma said God alone gave them such a blessing, and that the children of the Church could no longer follow the custom. It was not long before the custom was stopped.

She was very far out of the world, and seldom saw a white face. How glad she was when Mr. Bowes from Calabar appeared. They walked together from Ikpe to Odoro Ikpe. On the road she stopped and helped a woman to lift a very heavy load of palm nuts to her head. Then she went into the compound of an old chief who was ill, found out what was the matter, and arranged to send him medicine. At the entrance were three white chickens with their heads cut off. "It is a sacrifice," she said. "Oh, the pity of it." On going up the steep hill Mr.

Bowes wanted to carry a bag she had slung over her shoulder. "Na, na, laddie," she said, "it's my cat and it helps to balance me."

Writing to Ratcliffe at this time, she says:

> I have been without money for nearly a month! What do you think of that? Sometimes, but not very often, we have been hungry because we had not enough money to send to the market to buy food. The workmen make such a hole in my pocket. It is very difficult to get money brought from Calabar, and then the people won't take English money when it does come. They use copper wires, which we buy from the next station. Don't we live a very funny life? Pure gipsies, only we don't steal.

"It is sometimes a rather wearying kind of living, the gipsying sort of life," she told Christine; "but while there are no workers to go round we must do this as the second best way of holding on." And then she wonders what her little friend is doing and asks: "Are you going to do something fine in the new year? I trust so. At least you will be good, and To Be is a better verb than To Do in my estimation."

She began to remember that Christine was growing up, and did not like the idea. So she says to her: "I shall try and keep you in my heart with all the sweet mystery of girlhood. I should like, for many things, just to keep you among the simple loves and pleasures of home, and not to let you slip over into the womanhood which has such heights and depths that alternately beckon and frighten one. But God's order is the only right one, and you have a claim on Him."

"I shall be fifteen this August," Christine replied. "I am rather sorry we are all getting so big. However, there is one comfort, when we grow bigger we will be able to go out into the world and do good things, and perhaps splendid things, and help to make people better and happier—though, of course, we can do that always."

That was what Ma liked to hear, and when any of her young friends grew up and married and went out into that world of which Christine spoke, she would send them lovely messages. Here is one to a grand-niece of Mr. and Mrs. Goldie (the pioneer missionaries of Calabar who had been so good to her) when she was about to sail to America:

MY DEAR LASSIE—You do not know me, but your parents and all belonging to you are very dear to me, and I have always, from before you were born, loved you all and tried to follow you all.

And now God is calling you to live your life and to witness for Him in a strange land; and doubtless you will have fits of home-sickness, and times when you will want those who have hitherto made your world for you, and sometimes your husband will feel the same, for marriage does not—if it be a wholesome and sane one—destroy the old loves, but as one who knows what the leaving home means, I know that you will find your Saviour *near*, and *all-sufficient* for all times and things.

Do you know a good old practice of ours in a strange land has been to sing the second Paraphrase every Saturday night. You tell your husband to try it. At worship every Saturday night you sing that, and though your voices break, you will find it a tonic.

You will have all your things packed up and ready and your purchases all made, but as there are always a few small odds and ends, as hairpins and button-hooks, etc., left at the end when you are ready to embark and your boxes not at hand, I enclose a few shillings to have in your pocket for that emergency.

I remember Mrs. Goldie having forgotten gloves and safety-pins in Liverpool, and we rushed out of the cab to get them on our way to the steamer!

May every blessing go with you, and may your married life be a long and useful and happy one. He who hath hitherto led you will still compass your path.—Yours affectionately,

MARY SLESSOR.

Ma loved to hear how the girls at home were working for Jesus. How interested she was in all the new things that were being started—the Girls' Auxiliaries, the Study Circles, and Guilds! "The Church," she said, "is wise in winning the young, for they are going to be the mothers of the future and shape the destiny of the nation, and they will be all the wiser and the better mothers and Church members and citizens for what they are doing."

Some of her little friends were quite young. There was Dorothy, for instance, who was only five. She sent out Ma a picture-book which she had made herself, and Ma wrote back saying, "I wish I could give you a kiss and say 'Thank you' to your very real self by my very real self, instead of sending you a mere message on paper. But you see I cannot fly over the sea, and you can't come here, so what better can we do?"

The letters from home Ma kept, along with other treasures, in an old chest of drawers that she loved because it had been her mother's. If the bairns had been extra good she would gather them about her there after the lamp was lit, and show them everything. The letters were read over and over, and the children knew all about Dorothy's doll that could speak and sleep, and Jim's rocking-horse which Santa Claus had brought, and the new little brother that had come to Mary's home. Then the photographs of Dorothy, and Fay and her brother, and Christine and Happy, and others would be spread out and talked about and admired again. There were also the little gifts sent to her, just trifles, but very precious to her, because some bairn at home had worked at them. "To think of the trouble they took," she would say.

And the heather! How Ma loved it! These dry bits of plants brought tears to her eyes and sent her thoughts away across the wide sea to the homeland, and she saw in vision the glint of the sun, and the shadow of the cloud on the purple moors, and felt the scent of the heather and the tang of the salt sea breeze, and heard again the cry of the whaup.

"That's the Bonkle heather," she would say; "oh, the kind hearts there." "And that's the Blairgowrie heather and bog myrtle; never a year but it comes, and it is like a call across the sea."

One package she opened very tenderly, for it held the wee toys and well-worn books of a little boy who had died. They had been sent out to her from the heart-broken mother. Ma could never look at this beautiful gift without her eyes growing misty with tears.

In another corner was a cupboard filled with china and coloured glass, very common, but very rare in Ma's eyes, because they were gifts bought by the bairns at market or factory with their odd pennies and shyly offered to her. She often scolded them well for wasting their money in such a way, but all the same she was proud of these tokens of their love.

Then, softened by sweet memories and kind feelings, the family went to evening prayers. The children, squatting on the floor, read verses round, and Ma talked to them simply about higher things, sometimes in Scots, sometimes in Efik, after which they would sing old psalms or hymns, like "Now Israel may say," which was one of Ma's favourites. No books were used, and woe betide the bairn or visitor who did not know the beginning of the next verse! Ma, however, liked the children to learn new hymns, and sometimes they could be heard singing the tuneful ones in the yard or away in the bush or on the road.

CHAPTER XI

What happened when the Great War broke out. Ma's last voyage down the Creek; how her life-long dream came true. Now she lies at rest, and dreams no more, but her work goes on.

THE house at Odoro Ikpe was nearly finished. It was August 1914, and strange stories were being whispered among the natives of a great war in the world of white men beyond the seas. Ma knew how swiftly news travels in Africa, and became anxious but did not show it, and went calmly about her duties. The people grew more and more restless and excited, food became dearer, and no lamp oil could be had. She had to read at night by the light of a wood fire.

One day she was sitting in the new house when the mail boy came running up with letters. She took the packet and read of the invasion of Belgium by the Germans, with all the horrors of that terrible time, the coming of Britain into the struggle on the side of right and justice and freedom. "Thank God," she cried, "we are not to blame."

But the dreadful news shocked and hurt her so much that she became ill and could not rise. The girls carried her over to the rest-house and put her into her camp-bed and for many days she was in a raging fever. At last, worn out, she lay in a stupor. Round her stood the house girls and some of the lads of the Mission weeping bitterly. What should they do? They felt they must not let their beloved Ma die alone so far away from her own people. They must take her to Use.

So they lifted her in the camp-bed and set out for Ikpe carrying her gently over the streams and up and down the hills. Next morning they put the bed into the canoe and covered up the shrunken form and the thin withered face. The yellow cat was also put beside her, but the bag slipped open, and it was so frightened that it rushed into the bush and disappeared. It could not be found, and there was not time to wait, for a long journey lay ahead, and so it was lost and never seen again.

All day the lads paddled down the beautiful Creek among the water-lilies, and at night they took her ashore at the landing-beach, and she lay in the white moonlight until medicine was got and given to her, and then they carried her over the three miles to Use. Thus she came to the only home she had, never to leave it again.

She became a little better, and was able to get up and move about, but all the old fighting spirit had gone, and she was very tender and gentle and sweet. The War troubled her, and she was always thinking of our brave soldiers in the trenches and praying for them. But she felt she could do nothing, and was content to leave everything with God. To a little boy and girl at home she said, "God will work out big things from the War, for there is no waste with Him." And to Christine she wrote, "Every blessing be yours in the year that comes. Though it opens in gloom there is Light on ahead."

Yes, for her, too, there was Light ahead. One night she lay dying in her mud-room with its cement floor and iron roof. Miss Peacock was with her and the girls, Janie, Annie, Maggie, Alice, and Whitie. Alice never left her, and slept on a mat beside her bed. Through the long hours they kept watch. Ma was restless and very, very tired, and sometimes begged God to take her home. Once a cock crew, and they drew aside the blind thinking it was day, but there was nothing but darkness. Just before dawn Ma's wearied spirit passed softly into the Unseen. The dream she had dreamed so long, that she might see her mother and sisters and brothers again, had also at last come true. But the people wept, saying, "Adiaha Makara is dead. What shall we do? How shall we live? Our Mother is dead!"

Once more she voyaged down the Cross River to Duke Town, and there she was buried on the Mission hill, all Calabar, young and old, turning out to line the streets and show their deep sorrow. At the head of the grave sat old Mammy Fuller, a coloured woman from Jamaica, a faithful servant of the Mission, who had welcomed Ma when she first arrived, a bright-eyed happy girl, thirty-nine years before, and had loved her ever since. Ma had been fond of her too, and said it was she who ought to have had the Royal Cross.

"Do not cry," said Mammy to the women who began to wail. "Praise God from whom all blessings flow."

There was sadness in many a little heart when the news went across the ocean that Ma was no more. Ratcliffe missed the letters that used to flash like rays of sunshine into his quiet life. What of that wonderful secret which he had kept so closely locked up in his heart? He was told that it was all right now, and that there would be no harm in telling what it was. It turned out to be very simple, like many bigger mysteries and secrets. Ma and he had agreed to pray every day that he might get better and be able to walk, and he was to be good and always do his best.

Ratcliffe has never forgotten that compact he made with Ma, and he believes that she is loving him, and praying for him still, and that her prayers will be answered. He is now in Liverpool attending a school, and can go about on crutches with greater ease—sometimes for two and three hours at a time. He can also use his tricycle better and enjoys a three- or four-mile ride.

Christine, too, mourned for the loving friend she had never seen, and as she remembered the black children left motherless and alone she felt their sorrow and cried their cry, and put it all into the music of a haunting lament, a beautiful poem, which begins:

> She who loved us, she who sought us
> Through the wild untrodden bushlands,
> Brought us healing, brought us comfort

Brought the sunlight to our darkness,
She has gone—the dear white Mother—
Gone into the great Hereafter.

Ma's death made her famous. She, who was always hiding herself in life, was written and talked about and praised everywhere. The story of her heroism, devotion, and faith made her known and admired in many homes throughout the world, and so, although she lies in a far-off tropical land with her hands folded in rest and her lips quiet for ever, she is still helping and inspiring many as she did of old.

She was a puzzling person in many ways. Perhaps her dear friend, Mr. Macgregor, describes her best when he says, " She was a whirlwind and an earthquake and a fire and a still small voice, all in one." But she was also from her childhood, a dreamer of dreams. Not day-dreams which fade away into nothing. Not dreams of the night which are soon forgotten. But the kind of dreams which grown-up people sometimes call ideals, dreams that have in them the purpose of doing away with all that is evil and ugly, and making the world happier.

Many young people dream dreams, but they do nothing more. Their dreams are like the clouds that drift across the summer sky and disappear. Miss Slessor would never have done anything if she had *only* imagined all her dreams. If a boy only longs to be a good cricketer or swimmer, he will never become one. If a girl only thinks about a prize at school, she will not gain it. If a sculptor or artist only dreams about a beautiful statue or painting, the world will never have the joy of seeing them. We have to set to work and make what we dream about a real and solid thing.

That is what the White Queen always did. Her dreams came true because she prayed hard and toiled hard and waited hard and loved hard, yes, and laughed hard, for faith and toil and patience and sympathy and humour are all needed to win success.

There was only one of her ideas which did not come to pass in her own time—her home for women and girls; and that she would have seen also if she had lived a little longer, for it took hold of the Church, and a great deal of money came in for it. It was like a bit of weaving which she had not time to complete. Young and old, who loved and admired her inside her own Church and elsewhere, took up the threads and finished it and made it a lasting memorial of her. A number of native buildings and a Mission House were built, and there, under the clever guidance of her old comrade Miss Young (now Mrs. Arnot), young lives are being trained in all the things that make girlhood and womanhood useful and pure and happy. And there, too, is a beautiful gateway where tired men and women and children travelling along the hot roadway take shelter from the sun, and rest, and find water to quench their thirst, and think, perhaps, of the Great White Mother who spent her life for their good.

The church at Ikpe built by Ma was destroyed by a falling palm tree; the house on the hill-top at Odoro Ikpe was blown down by a tornado, and part of the roof carried away into the valley; but her work goes on. Many of the young men she taught are now members of the Church; the services in all the towns are crowded; the schools are full of scholars, and others are being built.

Who is going to follow in Ma's footsteps, here and elsewhere?

She herself believed that it would be the young people of to-day. "I am glad to know," she said, "that the girls and boys are thinking of us and praying for us, and denying themselves and planning perhaps to come to our help."

Yes, the future of Africa, and, indeed, of the whole world of heathenism, lies with the young hearts who are dreaming dreams of what they are going to do in the days to come. They will, by and by, be the pioneers and workers in the dark lands across the seas. It is to them that Jesus is looking to bring about the time when the whole earth will be filled with His light and love and peace.

Every one, of course, cannot work in the Mission field, and we do not require to go there to be a missionary. Wherever you may be, whatever you may do, you can always be a missionary and fight as valiantly as Miss Slessor did against sin and wrong-doing. You may not find your task easy. Our heroine did not find hers easy

You may meet as many difficulties as Christian did on his pilgrim way, and your dreams may be laughed at and scorned, but if you trust Jesus and persevere, you will come out all right in the end.

Dream your dreams then brave ones, lovely ones, but be sure and do your best to turn them into realities, for it is only those that come true that are making life better and sweeter and shaping the world into beauty.

THE END

THE CALABAR MISSION OF THE CHURCH OF SCOTLAND

CALABAR, the scene of the life-work of Mary Slessor, is a province of the great Protectorate of Nigeria in West Africa. The Scottish Mission there was started in 1846 at Creek Town, on the Cross River. At first the work was difficult and arduous, but a footing was gradually secured and outposts opened in the interior. The change that has come over the scene during the past hundred years is little short of wonderful. The Presbyterian Church of Eastern Nigeria is now in being with 11,000 Communicants and 43 congregations. Its ministers are trained in the Theological College at Umuahia along with Anglicans and Methodists. There are 4 medical stations including Itu Leper Colony. African women are being trained as nurses. The Hope Waddell Training Institution is now a secondary school and has also an Industrial department. At Obanelu there is a Union Training College for women teachers and at Ibiaku a secondary school for girls.

The work of the Slessor Memorial School still continues and in the Goldie College, Arochuku, young African women are being trained as evangelists.

PRINTED IN GREAT BRITAIN FOR
HODDER AND STOUGHTON, LIMITED, BY
COX AND WYMAN, LIMITED,
LONDON, FAKENHAM AND READING